Strips, Toons, and Bluesies

Essays in Comics and Culture

D.B. Dowd and Todd Hignite, editors

Princeton Architectural Press, New York
Washington University in St. Louis

741.509
STR

Published by
Princeton Architectural Press
37 East Seventh Street
New York, New York 10003

For a free catalog of books,
call 1.800.722.6657.
Visit our web site at www.papress.com.

This book was originally published as a catalog
titled *The Rubber Frame: Essays in Culture and
Comics* to accompany the following exhibitions
at Washington University in St. Louis:

*The Rubber Frame: The Visual Language
of Comics from the Eighteenth Century
to the Present*
Special Collections Gallery at
John M. Olin Library
October 1–December 31, 2004

*The Rubber Frame: American Underground
and Alternative Comics, 1964–2004*
Des Lee Gallery
October 1–October 30, 2004

Support for this project was provided by
the Missouri Arts Council, the Regional
Arts Commission, and various units at
Washington University. For a complete listing,
please consult the acknowledgments on
page 111 of this book.

For Princeton Architectural Press
Project editing: Clare Jacobson
Special thanks to: Nettie Aljian, Dorothy Ball,
Nicola Bednarek, Janet Behning, Becca Casbon,
Penny (Yuen Pik) Chu, Russell Fernandez,
Peter Fitzpatrick, Jan Haux, John King,
Mark Lamster, Nancy Eklund Later, Linda Lee,
Katharine Myers, Lauren Nelson, Scott Tennent,
Jennifer Thompson, Paul Wagner, Joseph
Weston, and Deb Wood
—Kevin C. Lippert, publisher

Design: Plum Studio

Typefaces: Luminance, Transfer, and Berthold
Akzidenz Grotesk

Printing: The Stinehour Press

Library of Congress
Cataloging-in-Publication Data

Rubber frame
  Strips, toons, and bluesies : essays in comics
and culture / D.B. Dowd and Todd Hignite,
editors.
     p. cm.
  Originally published in 2004 under the title
The rubber frame; published in conjunction with
two exhibitions held at Washington University in
St. Louis: The rubber frame: the visual language
of comics from the eighteenth century to the
present, held Oct. 1–Dec. 31, 2004 in the Special
Collections Gallery at John M. Olin Library, and
The rubber frame: American underground and
alternative comics, 1964–2004, held Oct. 1–30,
2004 in the Des Lee Gallery.
  Includes bibliographical references.
  ISBN-13: 978-1-56898-621-0 (alk. paper)
  ISBN-10: 1-56898-621-1 (alk. paper)
  1. Comic books, strips, etc.—History and
criticism. I. Dowd, Douglas Bevan. II. Hignite, M.
Todd. III. Washington University (Saint Louis,
Mo.) IV. Title.
  PN6710.R83 2006
  741.509—dc22

                              2006008315

Cover images

Frank King, *Gasoline Alley*, Image reprinted
with permission of Tribune Media Services.
©1931 *The Chicago Tribune*.

Jaime Hernandez, panel from "Mechanics:
Part Two," *Love and Rockets* #7, page 6.
Image reprinted courtesy of Fantagraphics
Books. ©1984, Jaime Hernandez/
Fantagraphics Books.

Winsor McCay, detail from *Little Nemo
in Slumberland. New York Herald*,
November 4, 1906.

D.B. Dowd, animation still from samthedog.com
cartoon "Rocket Mutt," 2001. Image courtesy
of Sam the Dog, Inc. ©2001 Sam the Dog, Inc.

Demian Vogler, *When I am King*, Chapter 1,
Scene 4, detail. Interactive online graphic novel.
©2000 Damian Vogler.

Unknown Artist, "Adventures of a Fuller Brush
Man: Obliging Lady." Cover, Tijuana bible.
Publisher unknown. n.d.

contents

5 **Foreword**
D.B. Dowd & Todd Hignite

6 **Introduction**
Angela Miller

8 **Strands of a Single Cord:
Comics & Animation**
D.B. Dowd

34 **Two Centuries of Underground Comic Books**
Daniel Raeburn

46 **Jaime Hernandez's "Locas"**
Todd Hignite

60 **The 1960s, African Americans,
and the American Comic Book**
Gerald Early

82 **A Chronology of Comics
and the Graphic Arts**
D.B. Dowd & Melanie Reinert

107 **Selected Bibliography for Chronology**

108 **Image Credits**

110 **Contributors**

111 **Acknowledgments**

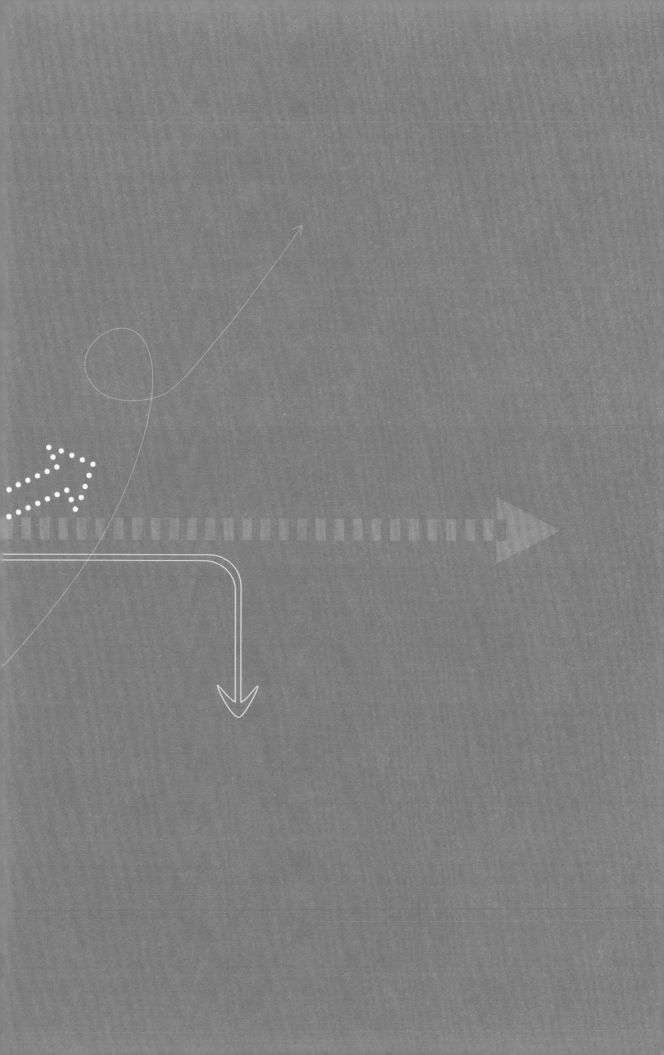

D.B. Dowd and Todd Hignite

This book seeks to engage comics with sympathy and grounding rigor. The dangers that attend the subject are well known. You can count them on three fingers: breathlessness, insularity, and persisting modernist snobbery. We acknowledge that much pioneering scholarship on the history of the medium has been produced by comics devotees. But the analytical limitations of fandom can pose significant problems. Hermetic encounters with comics lack the context of other graphic forms. Finally, high-cultural commentators have tended to view comics—precocious, but vulgar—as inky grist for real art: something mere. We offer this book as a modest, partial antidote. The essays to follow address the medium from multiple perspectives. The field of comics, a plastic subject if ever there was one, permits and rewards various approaches.

To support and overlay these multiple perspectives we have prepared a chronology of comics and the graphic arts, a densely layered and somewhat idiosyncratic timeline that we hope will, along with the essays themselves, make a contribution to the study and appreciation of the field.

This project has emerged from a curatorial undertaking in the history of comics. In the summer and fall of 2004 the editors of this book were engaged in presenting two exhibitions at Washington University in St. Louis: "The Visual Language of Comics from the Eighteenth Century to the Present," and "American Underground and Alternative Comics, 1964–2004." These exhibitions and an earlier edition of this book appeared under the overarching banner of "The Rubber Frame." Since that time, the subject of comics has attracted

growing attention. The blockbuster "Masters of American Comics" exhibition jointly organized by the Los Angeles County Museum of Art and the Hammer Museum at UCLA suggests that art historical methodologies will be brought to bear on these fundamentally popular materials. This project, which relies on more broadly cultural interpretive approaches, seemed to us and Princeton Architectural Press like a timely addition to the dialogue about comics. Hence this retitled and updated edition.

The editors wish to express sincere thanks to all who have supported this undertaking. ***Strips, Toons, and Bluesies*** provides evidence of growing scholarly commitment to popular visual culture and points to the emerging community of inter-disciplinary inquiry at Washington University in St. Louis. We gratefully acknowledge the support of the Missouri Arts Council and the Regional Arts Commission. Students from the Visual Communications program in the School of Art have played key roles in the production of this book. We invite the reader to turn to the acknowledgments page for a full accounting of the many individuals who have contributed to this complex and highly rewarding project.

introduction Angela Miller

In these years on either side of the new millennium, we face what must seem to those of less flexible mindsets a disturbing erosion of cultural categories. How to navigate a cultural landscape without the familiar markers of high and low, without the grounding distinctions between serious, critical, and reflexive art, on the one hand, and mass media on the other — "low" cultural forms long associated with facile formulas, soporifics for a public robbed of the ability to deal with complexity and irony? How also to understand a situation in which subcultural forms, from underground comics to hip-hop, have won mainstream acceptance? In which comic books — which many still associate with superheroes and adolescent fantasies — tell stories of the Holocaust and routinely adopt the self-critical and difficult address that, in the words of Clement Greenberg, "keeps culture *moving*" ("Avant Garde and Kitsch" 1939)? Comic artists such as Jaime Hernandez and Chris Ware now display many of the features thought to be peculiar to more sophisticated forms of modernism and postmodernism: irony, self-reflexivity, Brechtian alienation. Comics also comment on the internal history and framing conventions of their medium — playing around with the frame itself in endlessly inventive ways, translating the back and forth oscillations of time and memory, past and present, into graphic language. High art forms, conversely, adapt the features associated with mass forms — replication, repetition, formula, narrative — in their pursuit of the "non-auratic." Yet despite this tango of mutual seduction, the categories of high and low still retain a curious power over us.

The erosion of these familiar markers is part of the general historical shift known as the postmodern. But our postmodern moment has, like other periods of cultural change, stimulated us to reconsider the history of these forms themselves. In the last thirty years the history of comics has been rewritten, or perhaps written for the first time, as we discover that the current generation of extraordinarily fertile and inventive comic artists is grounded in a long history that at least matches it in graphic intelligence, historical depth, and self-reflexive humor. Searching for a useable past, historians and practitioners from Art Spiegelman to Daniel Raeburn have recovered Rodolphe Töpffer, Winsor McCay, Tijuana Bibles, and much more as they trace the surprising history of comics — now recognized as a sophisticated and self-knowing medium.

Comics were postmodern before the word was invented. They are about frames: frames as ways of narrating and composing time, ways of isolating moments in a temporal continuum, but also as a means of calling attention to how we know things. We know them because they refer to other things, as frames within frames — an endless *mise en abyme* that contains a good part of the history of visual communication. One of the beauties of the comic medium is its ability to use the conventions of the medium in ways that are easily understood on one level while at the same time subverting these conventions through parody. They are at once the most conventional and the most unfettered in their playful exploration of the form. Unlike the fine arts, this comic frame of meaning is more directly available. It is democratic in nature; it does not require a knowledge of arcane languages of criticism, highly private histories, or idiosyncratic experiences. It only requires participation in the community of those who read comics. And perhaps an understanding of, and curiosity about, the graphic and visual culture of the everyday. In reading comics, one enters a conversation that is welcoming but nonetheless demanding. One must pay attention. Much comic humor rests on its knowing engagement of other visual forms and cultural references: Rodolphe Töpffer transforms the earnest pseudo-science of physiognomy — the art of reading character from the face — into the springboard for his polymorphous imagination. Winsor McCay's **Little Nemo in Slumberland** delightfully expands on the prim conventions of polite children's literature; R.F. Outcault's children mimic the high-minded patriotism and silly class pretensions of adults. **Mad** comics parody the civil rights movement with reference to a history of race stereotypes that black activists had unknowingly reinstated.

It follows that reading comics does imply an initiated audience, composed of those who read comics (a nice tautology) and who have read enough of them to understand how they work. An audience of readers who love them, and who are ready to share their enthusiasms with those prepared to put aside their preconceptions. Yet as with any genre, comics have their share of bad. The misogyny of Robert Crumb without his inspired genius is just a cut above — or below — adolescent raunch. After the self-censorship within the comics industry, initiated by the Congressional hearings of the early 1950s, the underground comics movement of the 1960s unleashed a furious new license, unfettering the imaginations of comic artists with predictably mixed results. In tune with the counter-cultural impulse toward self-liberation and therapeutic freedom of expression, comics also found a new freedom to offend, which cut both ways, as Gerald Early's essay reveals. In going after the fantasy lives of repressed white people, comics traded in the racist content of those very fantasies with an anarchic force that far surpassed the boundaries of satire.

Yet comics at their best offer us privileged access to areas of experience off limits in most forms of everyday expression. Domesticated in the form of the daily newspaper strip, they are endlessly self-renewing, retaining their extraordinary power to penetrate the defenses of the socialized self, sometimes with lyrical grace, wit, and elegance — as in the fantastic journeys of Little Nemo into Slumberland — at other times vividly realizing fantasies perhaps better left bottled up. But in yet another expression of this wonderfully varied and rich medium, they also help shape group identities — be they ethnic, sexual, generational, or subcultural — through approaches that realize their subversively democratic potential. We need that now, at a time of growing corporate control over the images we live with, faced with the insidious new ways that globalized and consolidated media have found to colonize our psyches.

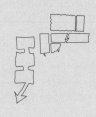

Strands of a Single Cord

Comics & Animation

D.B. Dowd

Graphic history is littered with singularities. Unlike art history, which has been laboriously constructed by philosophically minded big thinkers, the popular arts lack a unified tale. As a partial, unsatisfactory answer to this problem, each family in the graphic phylum — e.g., printmaking, caricature, illustration, comics, animation — has cobbled together an insular history before its own isolated hearth. The resulting multiple narratives invariably leave out much. Common influences are denied or ignored, and each clan tells a separate tale. Of all the graphic families, comics has developed the most complex historiography, a compelling story of itself. But the field can be powerfully inward looking. The story of animation, less complete and more dependent on technology, nonetheless has much to offer the tale being told around the comics campfire. Of primary concern in this essay will be the relation-ship between these two media. Comics and animation share founding affinities and intertwined origins. Challenges of production and problems of distribution have shaped the development of both fields. And recent technological change has fostered historic new creative and distributive options for artists and producers. Finally, the convergence of media and the intermingling of forms suggest a synthetic view of a larger subject. For the purposes of this essay, I will be addressing primarily American comics in the twentieth century. Japanese comics (*manga*) and *animé*, which have exerted considerable influence in the West, require sustained treatment precluded by considerations of length. My use of the term "animation" is meant to signify two-dimensional animation, or the draftsmanly version of the discipline. Stop-motion photography and CGI (computer generated imagery), or three-dimensional animation, fall outside the scope of my argument.

origins & affinities

Declarative statements concerning the origins of comics, or the origins of comic variants, are typically subject to dispute. The once unquestioned "fact" that R.F. Outcault invented the comic strip in 1896 on the pages of Pulitzer's **New York World** has been discredited. European sources from Rodolphe Töpffer (**Histoire de M. Jabot**, 1835) to Wilhelm Busch (**Max und Moritz**, 1865) to Marie Duval (**Ally Sloper**, 1867) provide prior examples of strip-like works of art.[1] Some of the earliest snatches of vocabulary for what would become the language of comics may be found in eighteenth-century intaglio caricatures by Hogarth, Gillray, or Rowlandson. The primordial stew of graphic form that winked into life as the first pictograph and evolved, incrementally, into **Dick Tracy** poses certain epistemological problems. Like who did what first where. I acknowledge, it's complex. But by any analysis, the creator of the Yellow Kid remains a significant figure.

R.F. Outcault displayed a gift for pictorial mayhem on the pages of the **World** in **Hogan's Alley**, the first

feature to incorporate the Yellow Kid. Each raucous, full-color episode was arrayed on a broadsheet with generous helpings of caption text sprinkled throughout. Two years later, in 1896 (having moved, with much fanfare, from Pulitzer's **World** to Hearst's **Journal**), Outcault added a comparatively spare, half-page comic strip called **The Yellow Kid**, arrayed in six panels, three up and three down.[2] The total result was a runaway hit and a merchandising bonanza. As a historical matter, if Outcault did not create the **Kid** strip *ex nihilo*, the various prior proto-comics cited above did not serve to inspire, outfit, and perpetuate something so durable as the four-color American Sunday newspaper supplement, either. Outcault fired the mass cultural and commercial launch — if not the formal or artistic one — of the comic strip.

R.F. Outcault,
"The Yellow Kid Indulges
in a Cockfight—
A Waterloo,"
The Yellow Kid.
Comic strip
(*New York Journal*)
November 29, 1896

 Eadweard Muybridge,
*Man Performing Back
Somersault.*
Series of photographs
1884

Winsor McCay,
*Little Nemo in
Slumberland.*
Detail of comic strip panel
(*New York Herald*)
February 18, 1906

But what of animation? The rapid evolution of the comics language from 1860 to 1890 betrays an accelerating artistic-industrial twitch, a broadly shared sense that things ought to get *moving* somehow. The "flipper" book (1868), Eadweard Muybridge's photographic motion studies (1877), Reynaud's praxinoscope (1877), even theatrical spectacles like the Gettysburg Cyclorama (1883) all reflect a growing impatience with the static image. Indeed, the early comic strip and its nineteenth-century antecedents share a preoccupation with capturing motion.[3] Busch and Duval, especially, revel in the drafting challenge of representing impossibly exaggerated yet comically plausible movements, anticipating the "stretch and snap" gags of the future animation trade. Shorthand indications of motion developed by late-century cartoonists are visible in Outcault's second *Yellow Kid* strip, concerning cock fighting; in particular, note the animated positions, "energy lines," and the spinning chickens in frame 4. So, by the time that Thomas Edison and his collaborator, cartoonist James Stuart Blackton, presented the first animated pictures, *Humorous Phases of Funny Faces*, in 1906,[4] the visual vocabularies for animated film — in the works for a generation, fostered by early comic strips — were finally at hand.

The twinned origins of comics and animation meet most vividly in the person of Winsor McCay, an illustrator, caricaturist, and poster designer who made his way to the *New York Herald* in 1903 via newspaper stints in Chicago and Cincinnati. McCay brought Freudian flair and Art Nouveau stylishness to his work in comic strips. He created a rash of them, most memorably *Dream of the Rarebit Fiend* and *Little Nemo in Slumberland* (beginning 1904 and 1905, respectively), both of which describe the unconscious adventures of a restive sleeper, in the former case due to an ill-advised bedtime snack of

Welsh rarebit. McCay was a graphic genius whose full-color *Nemo* strips astonish today, a hundred years later. For present purposes, what's most striking about McCay's comics work is that despite Little Nemo's fantastic adventures in mushroom forests, excursions to the moon, and trips to extravagantly silly royal settings, the comedy is grounded in physical fact.[5] In one memorable example, Little Nemo (a Little Lord Fauntleroyish, fussily attired boy) and Jungle Imp, an African playmate (a colonial-era McCay regular[6]), clamber over the New York cityscape, big as Japanese movie monsters. Leave aside the stunningly inventive scale shift; they really *clamber*. Or consider the headline banner of a *Nemo* episode reproduced here, spanned by a sequence of an acrobat in motion. The drawing instantly reminds one of the Muybridge studies. McCay was draftsman enough to invent anything at all, but he always brought even his most astonishingly plastic sequences — e.g., gigantic walking beds — back to the baseline questions of weight and mass, of physics. And physics would provide the iron laws of classical animation.

After 1910, as McCay's interests led him into pioneering experiments in animation, he applied lessons learned in comics, sometimes quite directly. Thus the *Rarebit* strip shown here, from 1909, provided the narrative spine for *How a Mosquito Operates* (1912), the second of his animated films after *Little Nemo* (1911). In the film, the giant, ravenous mosquito repeatedly feeds from the sleeping man's face. As the man intermittently rolls over and interrupts the insect, the latter is forced to manage an ever-filling sac of blood in his behind. As the sac grows heavier, the bug labors ever more strenuously to go back in for another nip. Like a drunken fat man on stilts, he rolls over on his back and struggles to right himself. Very simple stuff. And hilarious. Winsor McCay knew what Charlie Chaplin would come to know, too: that physical specificity makes things funnier. When Chaplin prepares a meal of boiled shoe in **The Gold Rush** (1925), he makes a serious effort to cut the sole with a knife and fork. It's heartbreakingly funny. But the physical *act* is funny, not the idea. So, too, with McCay's bug. (**How a Mosquito Operates** as a concept is quite *unfunny*.)

There is a final dimension to the early connection between comics and animation, an affinity of personality. The image of today's independent comic artist or graphic novelist tends toward the alienated sad sack. Not so with the likes of Outcault and McCay. Both were showmen, active players in the lucrative side business of "chalk talk," a vaudeville circuit for artists who performed with a crayon and a drawing pad before large audiences. McCay took chalk talk to a new level in 1914 when he produced an animated film, **Gertie the Dinosaur**, to integrate into his own live performances. The gigantic projected brontosaurus "carried" McCay away on her back to conclude the show. Crowds loved it.[7]

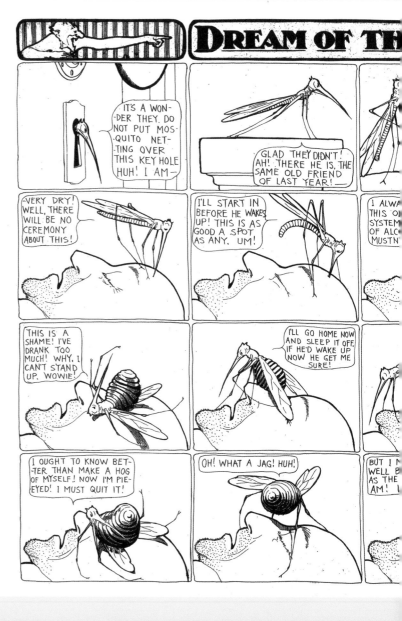

Winsor McCay,
*Dream of the
Rarebit Fiend.*
Comic strip
(*Evening Telegram*)
1909

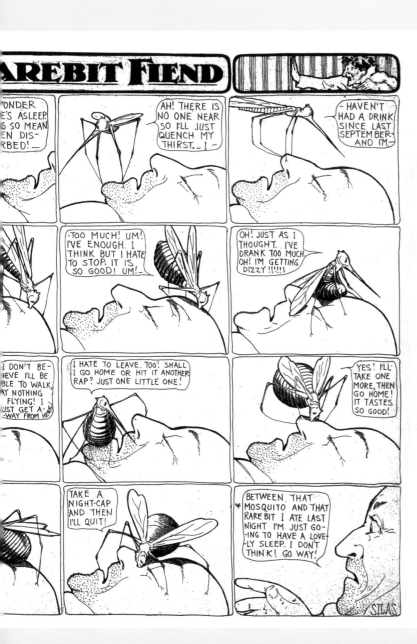

RESOLVED—
That we wear
BUSTER BROWN
shoes in the movies.
BUSTER BROWN
TIGE
MARY JANE

Arthur Trimble as Buster
Brown and Doreen
Turner as Mary Jane.
Promotional photograph
for Brown Shoe Company
associated with one of the
Buster Brown Comedies.
(Universal Productions)
circa 1925–1929

16

A common, founding interest in the description of motion links comics and animation. But significant commercial realities have played a role in the development of both forms. Problems of production and distribution are basic to both enterprises.

Comics are descended from eighteenth-century caricature and nineteenth-century illustrated journals. Innovations in printing technology, including the invention of wood engraving (circa 1770), lithography (1798), and the relief halftone (1852)[8] increased the speed of production, lowered the cost, and broadened the audience for illustrated materials, leading to an explosion in the number of weekly periodicals published in Europe and the United States between 1850 and 1890.[9] For cartoonists, whose work typically appeared in illustrated journals, the development of large-circulation daily newspapers created a new market of unprecedented scale. Improvements in color printing drove the development of the color supplement in 1892, creating the distributive vehicle for the Yellow Kid and his progeny.[10]

Popular new comic strips and characters popped up in a wide variety of American newspapers after 1900. Outcault's new Buster Brown character debuted in the **New York Herald** in 1902. The first major McCay strip, **Little Sammy Sneeze**, was launched by the **Herald** in 1904.[11] Lyonel Feininger, future Cubist, developed **Kind-der-Kids** for the **Chicago Tribune** in 1906. And Bud Fisher's **A. Mutt** (later renamed **Mutt and Jeff**) debuted in the **San Francisco Chronicle** in 1907.

The newspaper content syndication business adapted easily to incorporate comic strips and cartoons. The first syndicates appeared in the 1880s, and began to distribute visual material after 1895. Large increases in newspaper readership combined with the growing popularity of comic strips established a significant foothold for the strip medium by 1910; by 1920, the comics page had become a national institution. Important strips were launched in the teens, '20s, and '30s (e.g., George McManus's **Bringing Up Father** [Hearst Syndicate, 1913], George Herriman's **Krazy Kat** [Hearst Syndicate, 1913], Frank King's **Gasoline Alley** [**Chicago Tribune**, 1918], Phil Nowlan and Dick Calkin's **Buck Rogers** [1929], Chester Gould's **Dick Tracy** [1931], and Milton Caniff's **Terry and the Pirates** [**New York News**, 1934]).[12]

Driven by innovations in the advertising industry, the comic strip migrated to the comic "book" format in the late '20s and '30s. At first limited to newspaper strip reprints, comic books evolved into a vehicle for original material in publications like **New Fun Comics** and **Detective Comics** between 1935 and 1939. Superman (**Action Comics** #1, 1938) and his colleagues drove the creation of an entirely new market for comics, serialized superhero adventure stories issued in biweekly form.

By World War II, both of the great distribution channels for the comics were in place. The newspaper syndicates controlled the supply of content to the comics pages of American newspapers, and a variety of pulp publishers based in New York City supplied comic books to dime stores and other retail outlets. A short-lived Depression-era format, the small, square Big Little Book, did not survive the 1950s.

The production of comics in a commercial context required skill and speed on the part of the strip artist, who more often than not worked alone, though the use of assistants and even full-blown shop production were also common from the beginning. The self-reliance of the strip artists can be connected to their status as auteurs or "creators,"

responsible for writing and drawing. For production purposes, the dailies required nothing more than a photostat of the original strip, drawn in black. The more complicated Sunday strips involved the production of color separations for each strip, typically prepared by others, either at the syndicate level or at the job printers who produced Sunday supplements for the newspaper industry. (The job printers provided an early source of commercial energy in the developing comic book business, especially as advocates for reprint premiums for the advertising industry.)[13]

Production in the mature comic book trade developed differently, for very corporate reasons. The independence of the strip artists became unknown in the realm of the superhero, especially in the aftermath of the Superman controversy pitting young Siegel and Shuster — inventors of the Man of Steel — against Harry Donenfeld's DC Comics. Comic

publishers were eager to define and defend their own intellectual property against the claims of creators. Divisions of labor were established to make credit more diffuse. Thus every book got a writer, a penciller, an inker, a letterer, and a colorist.

A case can be made that the division of labor in comic book production is not really necessary except as an asset protection strategy, though the publication schedule for major titles might suggest otherwise. No credible argument can be made against the necessity of divided labor in commercial animation, however.

The technical steps required to produce early animated films were few but daunting: *1)* the artist must produce a sufficient volume of drawings; *2)* the drawings must be photographed in sequence; *3)* the images must be shuffled through very quickly, as fast as twenty-four frames per second; and *4)* the moving image must be projected onto

a surface for public presentation. The mechanics of motion picture photography and projection, basic to steps 2, 3, and 4, were worked out through a competitive frenzy during the decades bracketing 1900. Thus, until the integration of sound in animated film (first accomplished in 1924 by the Fleischer Brothers, Max and Dave, popularized in 1928 by Disney's **Steamboat Willie**) the primary problem for the animator was an artistic one: that of conceiving, composing, and executing drawings.

Winsor McCay, working alone, generated approximately four thousand drawings to animate **Little Nemo** in 1911. For his extraordinary, lyrically grim 1918 propaganda film, **The Sinking of the Lusitania**, McCay and two assistants generated over twenty-five thousand drawings.[14] The labor challenge was considerable, even for the redoubtable Winsor, who approached the medium from an artistic perspective. In a commercial venture, which required a return on investment, a new approach would be necessary. Thus divisions of labor in animation developed in the suddenly burgeoning field from 1914 to 1915.[15] McCay's keenly draftsmanlike emphasis on weight, mass, and sophisticated movement would give way to the rubbery caprice of Felix the Cat, in part because the "gooseneck" style could be executed by brigades of lesser talents.

Animation made its first appearances in vaudeville shows, then migrated to the movie house. The complexity of the production process foreclosed the possibility of long formats. So the animated short was developed to play an introductory, warmer-upper role before the live-action feature. Otto Messmer and Pat Sullivan's Felix the Cat became an international screen star in the days before sound, then yielded the stage to Mickey Mouse and Walt Disney only after the latter figured out how to milk audio for laughs by treating the action musically, synchronizing the score to percussive events in a cartoon.

Major studios developed divisions to supply animated shorts to play with studio features in studio theaters. This arrangement served the art of animation brilliantly, insofar as it supplied animation groups (like the Warner Brothers unit, or UPA and Columbia) with capital they might not otherwise have secured. It played less well with the Justice Department, which challenged the vertical integration of the movie business by bringing **U.S. v. Paramount**, an antitrust action. The landmark 1948 **Paramount** Supreme Court ruling destroyed what remained of the studio system. The action weakened the market for theatrically released cartoons, and badly damaged the industry.[16]

Disney, which had pioneered the full-length animated feature with **Snow White and the Seven Dwarfs** in 1937, charged ahead with long format, realistically animated theatrical releases. Some studios continued to produce shorts in a depressed market; others sought advertising work.

Television saved animation in the late 1950s. Bill Hanna (**Ruff and Reddy**, 1957; **Huckleberry Hound**, 1958) and Jay Ward (**Rocky and his Friends**, 1959) adapted to new financial realities by developing production systems to produce longer format material — the television version of a "half-hour" being twenty-two minutes of content — at a lower cost. The resulting visual style, which stressed two-dimensional shape making, flat color, and similarly graphic background art, relied on minimal movement. (The beginnings of the "limited" animation style can be located in UPA's **Gerald McBoing Boing**, a 1950 short, and Disney loose cannon Ward Kimball's **Toot, Whistle, Plunk and Boom**, from 1953; both films won the Oscar for best animated short in the year they appeared.) Despite the early creative promise of limited animation, the emergence of the Saturday morning cartoon slot in the early 1960s created a nesting ground for increasingly mediocre material.[17]

From the beginning, the entertainment neighborhoods of comics and animation have been crisscrossed with traffic. Little Nemo and the gluttonous mosquito were born in comics and ended up in pioneering films. Fifty years later, Charlie Brown and friends migrated from the comics page to holiday television. In general, the animals among the comics crowd have tended to move into the animation business, while the people, from Buster Brown to Dick Tracy, have opted more often for radio and live action film. The opposing path has been trod as well. Felix and Mickey started life in animated film and moved, via corporate production shops, into syndicated comics and Big Little Books in the 1930s. As time has progressed, the wide spectrum of entertainment formats has come to absorb all manner of characters generated in the comics and in cartoons, from radio to interactive gaming.

technology & innovation

For an aspiring graphic artist in 1965, mainstream participation in the popular forms of comic strips and comic books would require a pair of significant accommodations: one, access to distribution would require adherence to prevailing tastes, and two, participation would involve active collaboration with an organization of significant scale, whether a syndicate or a comic book publisher. Mass popular forms require investment to finance production, to support sales and marketing budgets, to cultivate and nurture talent. In exchange, publishers and syndicates expect professional commitment and contractual acceptance of the rules of the game.

The topic sentence of the preceding paragraph would read just as plausibly if it began, "For an aspiring graphic artist in *1945...*" But by the time that Johnson beat Goldwater, the cultural stresses of the '60s were in play, acknowledged or not. Things had changed; the equation had been altered.

Mainstream comic book publishing was in flux. The Congressional hearings inspired by Dr. Fredric Wertham's **Seduction of the Innocent** (1954) had led to the self-censoring Comics Code Authority. The horror and crime comics that provoked the reforming psychiatrist had been worthy of objection, though Wertham's claims that such comics produced antisocial effects in the children who read them could not be supported by the plainly anecdotal evidence cited in his book. But the industry, spooked, kept its head down and promptly devolved. The superhero genre went stale, leaving the likes of Richie Rich, war comics, and goofy romances to brave the market. As it happened, Stan Lee and Jack Kirby re-imagined superheroes in 1961 for Marvel with the **Fantastic Four**, but even so, industry offerings remained variously tepid, juvenile, and corny.

Lots of people who had been in thrall to pre-code comic books as kids rejected the bland new product. As adults, a certain fraction of them aspired to produce long format comics, but not under the available terms. Official accounts suggest that the birth of the alternative comix movement (am I the only person who finds the willful plural of "comix" self-regarding?) occurred in 1967 in psychedelic San Francisco, through the efforts of Robert Crumb and others.[18]

Zap Comix and its ilk of the underground (Foolbert Sturgeon's *The New Adventures of Jesus*, 1964; Gilbert Shelton's **Wonder Wart-Hog**, 1966; and, in the formulation of Daniel Raeburn, evangelical comics by Jack Chick, circa 1962)[19] provide a founding imperative for self-publishing in comics that represents a break with standard methods of production and distribution, and also points to an incipient culture of amateurism. I hasten to add that significant self-publishing in illustrated fiction

is at least as old as Blake. But comics moved into the world of radical self-publishing — ultimately best represented by the advent of mini-comics in the 1980s — by virtue of several developments, including technological evolutions in photo-mechanical reproduction. Comic books had always been cheaply printed, but cheap is a relative term; large runs on high-speed offset presses are typically beyond the independent graphic artist, who can't hope to move a large inventory of this or that oddball comic.

The persistence of the mimeograph and development of xerography changed the economics of small print runs. Albert Blake Dick invented the mimeograph process in 1884. By partnering with Edison, the inventor launched a surprisingly long-lived enterprise; A.B. Dick Co. was manufacturing mimeograph machines as late as 1986. Many early underground comics were chunked out on old mimeographs in that telltale purple-blue duplicator ink. Electrostatic photocopying, a superior technology, was invented in 1938.

STRANGE SKIES

LESSON NO. ONE-

DREAMT: MAY 1 0 1989
DRAWN + WRITTEN: MAY 1 3 1989

 PIE JOHN P.

THE KIDS AROUND MY HOUSE WERE YELLING. I WENT OUT TO SEE WHY... THE SKY WAS FILLED WITH TERRIFYING OBJECTS...

ABOVE US A JUMBO JET WAS SLOWLY HAULING A STRANGE SHIP STRAIGHT UP...

THERE WERE TWO MOONS

THREE ZEPPELINS SLOWLY CROSSED THE ORANGE SKY

A PRIVATE PLANE CAME IN OVER THE LAKE BUZZING THE ROOFTOPS. I THOUGHT IT WAS GOING TO CRASH. IT WENT BEHIND MY HOUSE...

ONE

John Porcellino,
"Strange Skies,"
King-Cat #1.
Comic book panel
(Spit and a Half)
May 1989

Derek Kirk Kim,
Oliver Pikk #2.
Online comic strip panel
(www.lowbright.com)
2004
© 2004 Derek Kirk Kim

Panel 2: Oh, hello, Mary Annette! Glad I ran into you; I've been meaning to ask you a question. I know you don't know me that well yet, but I was wondering, if maybe... uh, if you got some free time later, um, maybe you'd wanna, uh... marry me?

Panel 4: Wait, wait! Before you say anything, please let me elaborate. I know what you're thinking. You think I'm just another slobbering fan who only loves you for your outer shell and celebrity status, right?

Panel 6: Well, I'm different. For although your physical self shines, it's the glorious light of your inner being that has pierced through the clouds of my heart. Plus, Ricky Martin only wants to shake your bon-bons. So, what do you say, Mary Annette?

Panel 7 (left): You need to get laid.

Gah! Have you ever heard of knocking?!

Panel 8: This isn't healthy, man. You're obsessed with her.

I am not! I was just, uh... I was just... I'm not obsessed with her!

Just don't hump the poster, you might get a paper-cut.

Get out!

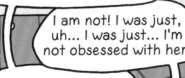

Panel 9: Okay, okay, I was just wondering where you were. *The Mary Annette Show* started ten minutes ago, and usually you're--

NNOOOOOO

known as alternative comics (join me in welcoming a normative plural back home), including those of Charles Burns, Gary Panter, and Chris Ware. The celebrated group of cartoonists and illustrators associated with **Raw** was headed for comparatively big-time publishing and distribution in the 1990s.

Things were different for the Kinko's crowd. New influences came from beyond the world of comics. Specifically, the DIY (do it yourself) movement in punk rock recording and publishing echoed Dadaist rejectionist stances on questions of quality and professionalism. The culture of the garage band brought a democratic casualness to what became known as mini-comics during the 1980s. As captured by Matt Feazell's stick-figure **Cynicalman** and John Porcellino's **King-Cat**, mini-comics emerge as writerly, private, odd, and visually informal. Porcellino, for one, constructs images that work verbally; they do more telling than showing. As a question of usage, "mini-comics" originally referred to the often pocket-sized books themselves, but the term evolved to suggest an enterprise of small scale. By virtue of a growing DIY ethic among young cartoonists, longer form comics, often pop*ular* but rarely pop*ulist*, began to move toward something more oblique, garrulous, and defiantly non-commercial. This process accelerated throughout the 1990s, as mini-comics attracted adherents and a growing number of primarily amateur practitioners. The range of content broadened over the same period, producing well-researched, richly visualized books like Dan Zettwoch's *Ironclad* (2002).[20]

My use of the term "amateur" should be considered ideological. Many of the cartoonists that I'd place under that umbrella are unschooled draftsmen, but just as many have received formal art training. I'm not

Xerox manufactured the first copier in 1949, and by the mid-'60s, photocopiers had spread throughout American office buildings. The institution of the local copy shop sprang up in the 1970s, and by the early 1980s truly affordable high-quality reproduction was in full bloom, via the flowering of Kinko's. Small runs, low material costs, and simple binding methods brought the activity of self-publishing within sensible reach.

The appearance of Françoise Mouly and Art Spiegelman's **Raw** in the 1980s launched or boosted significant careers in what became

Luc Jacamon and Matz, original graphic novel, Fons Schiedon, interactive adaptation. *The Killer,* adapted by Submarine Channel. Interactive online graphic novel based on *The Killer—Long Feu* (Casterman Editions, submarinechannel.com) 2001

using amateur as a synonym for *unserious*; rather I mean to capture the anti-professional stance implicit in the books. On a continuum of comics production values, with the most assured drawing, inking, and lettering at one end, and the most awkward stuff at the other, I'd put Milton Caniff on one end, and many mini-comics on the far one. Sometimes, the awkwardness is Brechtian and heightened, as in the work of Kevin Huizenga. Other times, it's simply crude, and unapologetically so.

That crudeness may be a reaction against ongoing advances in technology. The advent of personal computing brought significant change to commercial production. The release of Adobe Illustrator and Quark XPress in 1987 followed by the arrival of Adobe Photoshop in 1990 provided the graphic tools to produce and publish comics from the desktop. Mainstream publishers were quick to act on this potential, which aided coloring and provided an opportunity to replace hand lettering with computer typesetting. The boom in digital typeface design has resulted in a number of "comic" fonts for such use, but they have remained anathema to many. Chris Ware, the most analytic and designerly of the contemporary comic artists, has experimented widely with type. But the comics community, vulnerable like many to insularity, has largely rejected such innovations.

The diligence, commitment, and wit of today's mini-comic artists impresses. And despite a discomfort with the mainstream business and all it entails, the cartoonists are energetic merchants, in a medieval village sort of way. The transactions are many, eager, and modest. I'll confess that I find the attachment to hand lettering similarly medieval. In fact, the entire enterprise of non-mainstream comics has something hair-shirty and sectarian about it. It's true that the industry is a reliable supplier of dreck, just like all mass producers of popular art. But a certain percentage of all the variations on the not-Marvel-or-DC theme — underground, alternative, and mini; amateur and professional — share persistent motifs: brooding remembrances of childhood, a weakness for revenge fantasies, self-absorption, alienation, anxiety about authority, and an adolescent sense of melodrama. Comics can seem like an illustrated literature of loserdom.

Perhaps new developments and opportunities will have a bracing effect. The Internet, which evolved into a public phenomenon after 1995, has posed important distributive challenges for comics. Creators and publishers have produced a range of variations, certain of which extend, obviate the need for, or fail to match the print experience. Derek Kirk Kim (www.lowbright.com) provides the most basic example of a web-based comic, which is to say that the work appears online in a browsable form. *Oliver Pikk* is gag-driven and strip-like; *Same Difference* is a sixteen-chapter sustained narrative that unfolds vertically by virtue of an extended scroll from top to bottom. Kim storyboards well and draws beautifully, in a clear line style reminiscent of Hergé; the monochromatic tonal passages in *Same Difference*, applied digitally, are modest and evocative. Salon.com, an early adopter of online comic material, published a collaborative strip called *Dark Hotel*, written by Bob Callahan and drawn by Spain Rodriguez and others from October 1998 through November 2000. Each eight-panel episode can be viewed one panel at a time in a horizontal window inside the browser. Clearly, the viewing technology established parameters for the feature's composers. The designer solved the problem acceptably, but the format fails to satisfy the viewer, insofar as it cannot provide the simultaneous perception of interlocking whole and diverting individual part that we associate with a well-composed page of comic material.

The standardization of format that weakens *Dark Hotel* works wonders in Demian Vogler's *When I Am King* (www.demian5.com). This click-through horizontal "filmstrip" provides key frames or crucial drawings, leaving out the "in-betweens" that animation would require. The effect is something like a diagram for a silent movie. The clever tale (in which camels appear, notably, in pre-Columbian Mesoamerica), strong design, and vector-drawing style almost hold off the dawning realization that the work participates in the nineteenth-century proto-comics tradition, by using static drawing and serial presentation to communicate movement and tell a story. Here then is a case in which new technologies are employed to produce and deliver a work using old strategies and current aesthetics.

A final example leads us back to developments in animation. Submarine Channel, a Dutch new media concern, has sought to explore the evolving digital realm by developing and producing new media experiences, including online ones. Working with the artist and author of the graphic novel *The Killer*, a book-length comic by Luc Jacamon and Matz, in 2001 Submarine developed an online experience that used limited animation and canny sound design to present a hybrid experience of the original — sort of like reading, and sort of like watching and listening.

The overarching story I've sought to tell in comics traces the development of mass production and corporate distribution, answered by the birth of the independent producer and publisher. A very similar tale can be told in animation, and for comparable reasons: technological change in production

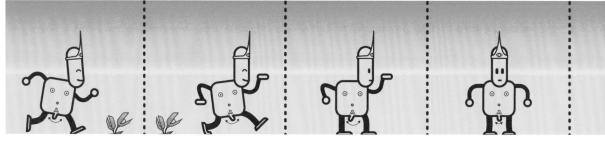

and distribution. Ongoing developments in personal computing,
including processing speeds and
computing capacity, have had a far
greater effect on animation than
comics. Before the mid-1990s, there
was no such thing as low-end
animation; even the limited animation
produced for television is exceedingly
expensive and is generally
animated abroad to control costs.
The development of motion graphics
software, specifically Macromedia

Flash 1.0 (released 1996), made it
possible to produce crude animation
on the desktop by using Adobe
Illustrator or Macromedia Freehand
vector images, which store graphic
information mathematically, thus
more efficiently than pixel-based
images, as in Photoshop.

Moreover, as new versions
of the software continued to appear
throughout the late 1990s, file
compression improved significantly.
File size mattered a great deal,

because in order to exploit the radically new distributive network of the Internet, a Flash file had to get small enough to "fit through the pipe," or be compacted into a small enough file size to be efficiently transmitted from a given website to a given computer. The phenomenon of online animation directly followed this development. (It's very important to note that much more sophisticated innovations in commercial 2-D animation occurred during this period, let alone the maturing of CGI [computer generated imagery, or 3-D animation]. The more pedestrian innovations of mere motion graphics concern us because Macromedia Flash made the production of inexpensive animation possible for the first time, and facilitated the use of a radically new distribution channel.)

Cable television opened up new frontiers for animation in the 1990s, which helped set the stage for the online animation boom. Fox, MTV, and Nickelodeon provided new outlets and opportunities for animated television shows, among them Matt Groening's **The Simpsons** (1989), Mike Judge's **Beavis and Butt-head** (1993), and John Kricfalusi's **Ren and Stimpy** (1991). In 1992, the Cartoon Network debuted with twenty-four-hour cartoon programming, a first. Entertainment industry players made early moves to exploit the online channel. Kricfalusi's Spumco (www.spumco.com) and Visionary Media's Whirlgirl (www.whirlgirl.com) offered the first online series in 1997.[21] As the Internet frenzy mounted, a legendary Marvel man entered the market with StanLeeMedia.com, an online entertainment company that would go down in history as one of the great Internet flameouts late in 2000, on the heels of a $25 million stock fraud (in which Lee was not implicated).[22]

The innovations in online animation did not come from the entertainment industry. Even by the standards of 1950s and '60s

limited animation, Flash files played online are extremely jerky and primitive. As a result, animators had to exploit sound and artwork to help obscure the simplicity of the animation. Almost all the best early examples are quite simple and sophomoric. Joe Cartoon's **Frog in a Blender** (1999) introduces interactivity to a potentially bloody encounter with a mouthy frog. Xeth Feinberg and Mike Reiss's ridiculous **Hard Drinkin' Lincoln** and **Queer Duck** (2000), both originally produced for icebox.com, use manic wit and an abiding stubbornness to wring as much humor as possible from modest gags, with mixed results. (Both are now viewable at Feinberg's mishmashmedia.com.) In the last few years, the field has matured a bit, yielding more varied results, including the work of Craig Frazier. Frazier, trained as an illustrator, given to a conceptual approach to image making, and known for visual puns, has produced stylishly animated pieces like **Pipedream** and **Greenville** at www.craigfrazier.com.

At the height of the Internet boom, Joe Shields (a.k.a. Joe Cartoon) was rumored to be making as much as $25,000 a month through banner advertising on his site. But online animation did not survive as a business. The excitement of affordable animation did not translate into profitable animation. So the process reverted to speculative work or job production for broadcast websites like CartoonNetwork.com, which are constantly in need of games and incidental content. So the online animators ended up like the mini-comic artists, except that they turned out to be unhappy amateurs, instead of ideological ones. That said, the still-maturing potential of the Internet, and the coming convergence of television watching, gaming, and computing suggests a promising future for animation. The future of the comics is less certain.

Considerable attention has been devoted to matters of production and distribution. But what are these things good for, after all? What function do these cultural objects and experiences fulfill?

Both comics and animation are thought to entertain — that is, divert — audiences of children and young people. This is largely true of animated movies and television shows, though they have sometimes sought to educate as well as entertain. And it's worth pointing out that the most successful animated programs are those which amuse kids and their parents at the same time. (The only really low point in the history of the medium occurred in the 1960s and '70s, when network programmers left the kids to languish with avowedly poor programming on Saturday mornings, since after all the tots wouldn't know any better.)[23] Whether movie or television program, longer format animation will also be focused on telling a story.

Long format comics tell stories as well. The mainstream books are aimed at kids; the alternative books and graphic novels address a slightly older audience. The kids will get fantasies of action; the adolescents will get riffs on alienation and other fantasies, both sexualized and macabre.

We have lost the trail of the newspaper comic for a time. Although compared with its origins, the contemporary comic strip is an ossified, talky, surprisingly nonvisual affair, the strips and the syndicates remain in the game. The comics play an important ritual role for many people, and provide a girding chuckle at the outset of the day. But the strip has been reduced to a joke delivery system. Arguably that's been true for a long time, since the disappearance of the continuity strips years ago. The cultural enterprise of the syndicated comic strip seems to attract fewer significant talents now, and the drawing grows thinner

and more graphically naive every day. The swashbuckling visual bravura of Winsor McCay is totally inconceivable now, and was last hinted at by the rich dinosaur fantasies and spaceship dramas — McCay homages, to be sure — that riddled the run of Bill Watterson's *Calvin and Hobbes*.

But comics in newspapers have also played an editorial role. Features like Garry Trudeau's *Doonesbury* and more recently Aaron McGruder's *Boondocks* sit uneasily in the laff riot comic section, though each provides amusement. Walt Kelly's *Pogo* had editorial points to make on nearly a daily basis.

The opportunity to produce editorially tinged entertainment drew me to newspaper work in 1997. At the invitation of editor Cole Campbell and editorial page editor Christine Bertelson, I developed a serialized illustrated satire for the *St. Louis Post-Dispatch* called *Sam the Dog*. Not really a comic, but amply illustrated, the weekly feature poked fun at contemporary self-satisfactions. The layouts were quite plastic from week to week; I was not subject to the iron format constraints of a strip. At the completion of the run, *Sam* moved from the *Post-Dispatch* to SamtheDog.com in 1999. Like many other people, I was drawn to the frontier of multimedia. Yet the challenges of animation, intoxicating at first, yielded a surprising discovery. Due to the necessarily abbreviated length of the average online animation — a function of the need to keep the file size small, so as not to clog the data pipe — the cartoon had to deliver a joke, simply and quickly. The visual sweep and editorial reach of the print feature simply wouldn't fit. Thus I left static print work for the more plastic world of online animation, only to find myself making talking comic strips.

In the late 1990s, Universal Press Syndicate (today, along with King Features, United Media, and Tribune

D.B. Dowd,
*Holiday Moments
with Cockeyed Neil.*
Macromedia Flash
animation still
(SamtheDog.com)
2000
© 2000 Sam the Dog, Inc.

D.B. Dowd,
Sam the Dog in
The Frame Job #78,
"The Arraignment."
Newspaper illustration
(*St. Louis Post-Dispatch*)
November 28, 1998

THE Honorable SILLY GOOSE *puffed herself up into a FEATHERED BAG. "Bring on the next one!"*

Judge Goose presided over the Trapper City Court of NORMATIVE JUSTICE. "The most important word of all," she was fond of saying, "is SHALT! As in SHALT and SHALT NOT." Day after day, Judge Goose enforced her shalts with an inexhaustible DIM FURY.

Sam the Dog was brought before Judge Goose. "Your exaltedness," he offered, "there's been a mistake--" An enormous BAILIFF stamped on Sam's foot. YOW! "Next, your divineness," boomed the bailiff, "THE PEOPLE v. SAM THE DOG." An EXCITABLE REED of a Prosecutor rose from his desk and shrieked, "I'll tell you what, judge--he's a killer! He shot Hoofer Dupree, dead!" Silly Goose frowned & peered at the handcuffed figure below her. "Sam the Dog," pronounced the judge, "you have been accused of murder. WORSE, people are claiming that your ideas are OUTSIDE the MAINSTREAM. How do you plead to these charges?"

"UM," Sam

began. "I don't really HAVE any ideas, your regalness. And I didn't kill anybody." The judge honked impatiently. The Prosecutor made an expectant sound, then proclaimed, "THE STATE WILL SEEK 17,000 VOLTS."

Media Services, one of the remaining major newspaper syndicates distributing comics) took a step to explore the future of comic strips and comic-like material in a digital environment. Universal management created and secured capitalization for a new company called *uclick* to manage the online presence of Universal's comics, and to develop new creators and properties for the online channel. The range of potential content was broad, from interactive crossword puzzles to animated editorial cartoons to gag-oriented animation. In theory, multimedia projects and characters would build audience via the *uclick* website and possibly later move into print. Felix and Mickey had moved from film to newsprint sixty years earlier. Why not? Now we know that the Internet speculation bubble obscured commercial problems that even today have yet to be worked out — most fundamentally, how will animated content producers generate sufficient revenue from the Internet? At the time, Internet content companies were banking on income from banner advertising, the rates for which had begun to collapse. Meanwhile, *uclick* was exploring relationships with — among others — **Washington Post** editorial cartoonist Pat Oliphant and animator

29

Steve Whitehouse (creator of the redoubtable **Mr. Man**), the latter a speedy independent with a great gift for limited animation and sound.[24] At SamtheDog.com, we were in the process of finalizing a contract with *uclick* in February 2001 when the ongoing financial collapse of the Internet finally rolled into Kansas City. All pending projects were cancelled.

Today *uclick* manages a solid business in online subscriptions, and has successfully entered the wireless communications market. The twenty-first-century commercial convergence of comics and animation has not yet occurred, though surely it will, because quick-hitter animation and the dogged form of the comic strip share a basic function — to make people laugh on short notice. That will probably be enough.

Little things are falling into bigger things. The consolidations of contemporary life seem inescapable.

Finally my thoughts are synthetic ones. Comics and the animated cartoon and the motion picture are strands in the same cord. The intermingled influence they have brought to modern visual culture can be difficult to untangle. Early experiments in comics created new ways to visualize movement. Walt Disney invented the process of storyboarding films, drawing out the scene before the fact. Hergé and others brought cinematic technique to comics. Winsor McCay imported the aesthetics of circus poster design to **Little Nemo**. N.C. Wyeth's Scribner's Classics illustration cycles influenced pictorial staging in adventure strips. Illustrator Lauren Redniss draws on the graphic

conventions of the speech balloon and all-caps comic typography to create a hybrid editorial image. Chris Ware brings the narrative sophistication of information design to the construction of his comic pages. The resonance of these visual rhymes and sources suggests a bigger story than the comics clan often tells. Distinctive areas of production remain, to be sure. Differentiation matters. Synthesis matters more. ☀

Steve Whitehouse,
Mr. Man: Fishing.
Macromedia Flash
animation still
(whitehouse
animationinc.com)
2003

Lauren Redniss, creator,
Steven Guarnaccia,
art director,
Laman and Loay.
Op-Art illustration
(*New York Times*)
June 3, 2003

notes

1   For a sustained treatment of European antecedents to the modern comic strip, see David Kunzle, *History of the Comic Strip*, vol. 2, *The Nineteenth Century* (Berkeley: University of California Press, c. 1990).

2   Outcault seems to have been slow to embrace the secondary feature. The greater visual opportunities lay in the full-page spatial/narrative extravaganzas of *Hogan's Alley* (retitled *McFadden's Flats* in the *Journal*), which may explain why the half-page comics appear less frequently after initial appearances in 1896 while the bigger production numbers continue through the Yellow Kid *World Tour* series of 1897. For an extended treatment of Outcault, the Yellow Kid, and New York newspapering in the 1890s, see Bill Blackbeard, *R.F. Outcault's The Yellow Kid: A Centennial Celebration of the Kid Who Started the Comics* (Northampton, Mass.: Kitchen Sink Press, 1995). For the narrower question of the multi-panel strips, consult chapter 9 of that book, "First Balloon Trip to the Rainbow: Outcault's Accidental (and Unnoticed) Invention of the Comic Strip," 69–76.

3   For an extended discussion of the graphic language of movement, see Kunzle, chapter 15, "Movement Before Movies," 348–375.

4   For a brief timeline on developments in animation technology see Richard Williams, *The Animator's Survival Kit* (London and New York: Faber and Faber, 2001), 11–20.

5   John Canemaker plausibly compares the unfolding adventure of *Slumberland* to works by Lewis Carroll and L. Frank Baum. Both the Alice and Oz cycles provide delightful, episodically structured discoveries of new worlds. John Canemaker, *Winsor McCay: His Life and Art* (New York: Abbeville Press, 1987).

6   Impy and his brethren first appeared in *Tales of the Jungle Imps*, McCay's *Cincinnati Enquirer* cartoon feature of 1903. The "savage" figure was but one of a host of African and African American stereotypes that remained common in newspaper comics through the 1920s and into the '30s. Gerald Early's essay in this book explores Robert Crumb's disturbing use of such stereotypes in the 1960s. A side note: the physiognomy of Impy, Nemo's frequent sidekick, closely resembles that of Bill Watterson's Calvin, of *Calvin and Hobbes* (Universal Press Syndicate, 1985–1995). As noted elsewhere in this essay, Watterson makes homage to McCay via fantastical scenes in Calvin's imagination. I suspect that the structure of Calvin's head is partly modeled on Impy, especially in the conventionalizing of the jaw and mouth.

7   John Canemaker, in voiced-over commentary on *Winsor McCay: The Master Edition*, dir. Winsor McCay (originally filmed 1911–1921), prod. Anke Mebold, Milestone, Cinémathèque Québécoise, 2003, DVD.

8   For a discussion of the implications of these new printing technologies, see William N. Ivins, Jr., "The Tyranny Broken: The Nineteenth Century," in *Prints and Visual Communication* (Cambridge, Mass., and London: The MIT Press, 1969), 93–112.

9   The scale and significance of these developments are well described by Paul Jobling in "A Medium for the Masses I: The Popular Illustrated Weekly and the New Reading Public in France and England During the Nineteenth Century," in *Graphic Design: Reproduction and Representation Since 1800* (New York: Manchester University Press, 1996), 9–40.

10 H.H. Kohlsaat's *Chicago Inter-Ocean* was the first American newspaper to print from a four-color press, during the Chicago World's Fair in 1892. New York papers followed suit the following year. The *New York World* published its first color supplement on May 7, 1893. Blackbeard, "Death of a Legend: The Great Yellow Ink Hogwash in M'Googan Avenue," chap. 4 in *R.F. Outcault*, 32.

11 A short-lived McCay strip, *Mr. Goodenough*, preceded *Little Sammy Sneeze.* See Canemaker, 63.

12 See Bill Blackbeard and Martin Williams, eds. *The Smithsonian Collection of Newspaper Comics* (Washington, D.C.: Smithsonian Institution Press; New York: Harry N. Abrams, Inc., 1977).

13 See Ian Gordon, "Comics as an Independent Commodity," chap. 6 in *Comic Strips and Consumer Culture 1890–1945* (Washington, D.C., and London: Smithsonian Institution Press, 1998), 129, on the invention of the comic book.

14 John Canemaker, in voiced-over commentary on *Winsor McCay: The Master Edition*, discusses the production process for *Lusitania*.

15 Karl Cohen, "Milestones of the Animation Industry in the 20th Century," *Animation World Magazine* 4, no. 10 (January 2000): 16.

16 Jason Mittell, "The Great Saturday Morning Exile: Scheduling Cartoons on Television's Periphery in the 1960s," in *Prime Time Animation: Television Animation and American Culture*, Carol A. Stabile and Mark Harrison, eds. (New York: Routledge, 2003), 35–36.

17 Mittell, 33–54.

18 Daniel Raeburn subjects the standard account to cross-examination in "Two Centuries of Underground Comic Books," another essay in this anthology.

19 Raeburn sheds fascinating light on Jack Chick's fundamentalist comics in his essay. He makes a persuasive case that Chick qualifies as an "underground" comic artist, in part because the narratives make use of certain conventions of pornography; taboo breaking or illicit content is a hallmark of the underground aesthetic. I would argue that for hip, thoroughly secular audiences, Chick's evangelical content and religious zeal can be seen as illicit: an intriguing inversion of the traditional equation.

20 Full disclosure: Dan Zettwoch was once a student of mine in the Visual Communications program at the Washington University in St. Louis School of Art, and I have followed the development of his career with interest. *The Comics Journal* has called his work "the biggest surprise of the last few years in mini-comics circles" (*TCJ*, no. 259 [April 2004]: 109). Zettwoch brings a more designerly approach to the construction of a page than do many in mini-comics, evident in the fold-out extravaganzas of *Ironclad*, an unlikely treatment of the historic battle between the *Monitor* and the *Merrimac*, and in the pocket-sized *Redbird* series.

21 Cohen, 23.

22 Jon Swartz, "Comics Exec Focuses on 'Spider-Man 2' as Former Partner Prepares for Trial," *USA Today*, 12 May 2004, B1.

23 Mittell, 41–42.

24 Chris Pizey (CEO of uclick), interview by the author, 18 June 2004.

Two Centuries of
Underground Comic Books ...

Daniel Raeburn

▶ We all know what underground comics are, or at least we think we know. They're "comix" from the late 1960s and early '70s that are full of sex, violence, and taboo breaking. Comics historians will tell you that these were the first comics to smash the status quo and stick it to The Man. At least that's the mythology. In his 2002 book, *Rebel Visions: The Underground Comix Revolution, 1963-1975*, Patrick Rosenkranz runs through the conventional wisdom, which is that the underground comics "movement" began in February 1968 when Robert Crumb started selling *Zap Comix* #1 out of a baby carriage on Haight Street. Rosenkranz also dates the movement to 1964, when Foolbert Sturgeon (a.k.a. Frank Stack) started hawking *The New Adventures of Jesus* in Austin, Texas. But Rosenkranz notes that another Texan, Jack Jackson, was selling *his* religious parody, *God Nose*, at the same time as Sturgeon. Rosenkranz also concedes that a surfing comic book from 1963, done by Rick Griffin, the Grateful Dead poster artist, could reasonably be called the first underground comic. Rosenkranz's goal is to show how pinpointing the origin of underground comic books is difficult. And he's right about that. It is confusing,

especially if you believe in the conventional wisdom, which I do not. I don't think underground comics began in the 1960s and I don't think they ended a decade later. I propose that we redefine the term "underground comics" to include a wider range of creators, idioms, and eras: First, in order to bring a more historical perspective to what is in fact a centuries-old tradition – illicit comic books were around long before the 1960s. Second, to point out that these underground comix were not that underground. By 1970, the books that are commonly accepted as "underground" comix were easily available, sold in head shops, sex shops, and other countercultural businesses, at a time when the counterculture was a fairly mainstream phenomenon. In the early 1970s the average underground comic book sold 40,000 copies. Today, the average "alternative" comic book sells around 4,000 copies, or one-tenth of its boomer ancestors, which makes today's alternative comics, quantitatively speaking, more "underground" than the undergrounds.

Third, the narrow definition of "underground" comics ignores too many other groundbreaking comics, starting with those of Rodolphe Töpffer, a Swiss writer who around 1830 basically invented the medium itself. Töpffer made his first comic book by hand in an edition of one copy – as underground as can be. Until recently, however, mainstream comics historians have completely ignored Töpffer. One hundred years after Töpffer came the Tijuana Bibles, also known as "eight-pagers," "bluesies," or "fuck books," which were sold across the United States. These comic books smashed just as many taboos as their '70s grandchildren and they did so in only one-fourth as many pages. Nobody knows who made the Bibles, so they're probably the most underground comics of all time. Of course, they too are generally ignored by the canonical histories of comics. The fundamentalist Christian cartoonist Jack T. Chick started making his own comic books as early as the 1950s. Since then Chick has built a worldwide volunteer network that has distributed over five hundred million copies of his comic books. So he is by far the most widely read underground cartoonist of all time. Yet he is almost never mentioned in any history of comics, underground or otherwise.

Rodolphe Töpffer (1799–1846), a Swiss prep-school teacher and essayist, is not only the creator of the first underground comic book; he is the inventor of comic books, period. He discovered this most disreputable art in the 1820s as he was studying physiognomy, which was fashionable at the time along with its cousin, phrenology. Töpffer found no science in this buncombe, but he did find an art. Basically, he found stereotypes, and lots of them. These stereotypes, he argued, provided a set of artistic tools that the caricaturist could use to outline a character. To prove this, Töpffer drew a head and systematically altered one feature at a time, showing how each iteration would change the reader's perception of this character. What made Töpffer's observations rise above the level of caricature was his suggestion that the artist not only use these physiognomic signs in combination to build character, but that he use them in sequence to tell a story. By doing so, Töpffer took the already popular format of the illustrated story to a new level, that of comics.

One of Töpffer's friends, who was living in Germany and taking care of Johann Wolfgang von Goethe, borrowed the originals for two of Töpffer's comics and showed them to the colossus of German letters, who was on his deathbed. Goethe loved them. "This is really too crazy," he said. "[Töpffer] really sparkles with talent and wit. Much of it is quite perfect. If, for the future, he would choose a less frivolous subject and restrict himself a little, he would produce things beyond all conception." So there you have it: the first review of the first comic book, spoken by the most famous critic in Western Europe.

Upon hearing this news Töpffer began producing his comics in small, limited editions and selling them for ten francs apiece to Swiss and French sophisticates. Soon his first book, **The Loves of Mr. Old Wood** (**Les Amours de M. Vieux Bois**) — about an old man trying in vain to woo a young woman — was the toast of the salons. (It's ironic that the salons took to these clever, somewhat risqué comics, because Töpffer always made a point of saying that his "picture stories" were ideal for children and the uneducated lower classes.) A well-known French publisher, Aubert, hired an artist of lesser talent to redraw **Old Wood** and began selling their swipe for six francs apiece. To combat this, Töpffer printed up some of his other comic stories and lowered his price to six francs. Of course, Aubert immediately swiped these comics as well. Töpffer protested this rip-off in an essay, which prompted Aubert to not only swipe all of Töpffer's comics but to rename their entire line of comic books Editions Jabot, after Töpffer's most popular character, Monsieur Jabot. Then the British got in on the act. The Fleet Street firm of Tilt and Bogue plagiarized the already bogus French version of **Old Wood** and sold their bastard version, entitled **The Adventures of Mr. Obadiah Oldbuck**, throughout the United Kingdom. In 1842, Wilson and Company of New York reprinted **Oldbuck** as a supplement to their humor magazine, **Brother Jonathan.** The American **Oldbuck** was a bootleg of a translation of a bootleg, sold for the exorbitant price of thirty cents and printed on that favorite substance of 1970s cartoonists, hemp, making it not only the first American comic book but the first American underground comic book. A recent book by two European scholars, Pascal Lefèvre and Charles Dierick, tells the story of this phenomenon and is entitled, appropriately enough, **Forging a New Medium**.

töpffer

London: Tilt and Bogue, Fleet Street.

Rodolphe Töpffer,
Hand-colored
advertisement depicting
the title page of
*The Adventures of
Mr. Obadiah Oldbuck.*
circa 1842–1843

Rodolphe Töpffer,
American edition of
*The Adventures of
Mr. Obadiah Oldbuck.*
Book (Dick & Fitzgerald)
circa 1870s–1888

As we've seen throughout history, beginning with the invention of the printing press, then with the camera, motion pictures, VHS, DVD, and the Internet, every time a new medium or technology comes along you can count on the pornographers to be right there, exploiting the leading edge. Comic books were no exception. In the first half of the twentieth century a group of unconnected or loosely affiliated American artists, working anonymously, wrote and drew an estimated seven hundred to one thousand different issues of so-called "Tijuana Bibles." At their peak in the 1930s these comics were printed by the millions and sold illegally like marijuana and moonshine.

Although these comics did stereotype gays and lesbians, they at least acknowledged their existence. I hate to disappoint our legislators and our President, but these comics make it clear that so-called "alternative lifestyles" were every bit as common back then as they are now. If it was illegal in Georgia and Mississippi, it was usually happening by page 4, page 6 at the latest. By page 8 you occasionally had a whole mess of people piling in on the action. Although group sex and homosexuality were more or less in the closet and under the rug, these comics prove that it was just as normal then as now. They also make it clear that people's sexual fantasies were the same then as they are now. The iceman and the brush salesman may have been replaced by the UPS guy and the bicycle messenger, but these comics prove that, even then, class tension was somehow bound up in our national sexual psyche. The typical Bible consists of a pampered, white housewife meeting a brawny immigrant worker and seducing him, or vice versa. Because these comics were sold primarily to working-class people and teenagers, the underdog usually came out on top, often literally.

Tijuana Bibles were also the first meta-comics. Many of them were about comics as much as they were about sex. Since comics were the TV of their time (a Gallup Poll taken in 1938 found that 70 percent of all adults followed the newspaper comics "faithfully"), it was only natural that these sex comics would use the stars of their time — Jiggs and Maggie, Popeye, Little Orphan Annie, even Betty and Veronica — to play the starring roles. What this did was point out the sexual undertones masked in the strip being parodied. It didn't take an Austrian psychologist to guess what was really going on with Batman keeping his ward, Robin, living in a cave, both of them served by Alfred the Butler, or why the billionaire widower, Daddy Warbucks, would adopt a cute little girl to live with him. This meta-comical aspect is why the Tijuana Bibles are not, ultimately, pornography. If the goal of por-nography is to sexually excite the reader, then these comics failed

miserably. Their real goal was satire. These comic books were not cheap. They cost a dollar or more even during the Great Depression, an extravagance for the generally poor people who read them. Yet these comics were as popular as corn liquor and its attendant Hell. In such lean times, millions of people were not paying a premium to see Minnie and Mickey screw in order to masturbate. At least I hope not. They paid a dollar in order to mock Walt Disney. And they did not pay a dollar for comics about Joe Stalin, Adolf Hitler, and Chambers and Hiss in order to learn more about foreign policy. They purchased these comics to try to have a laugh at the modern world even as its greatest horrors were inexorably gathering.

I make no grand claim for the political and cultural importance of these booklets. After all, they're just fuck books. But these little Bibles are a small, missing link in the evolution of parody and satire in American pop culture. Art Spiegelman wrote, "Without the Tijuana Bibles there would never have been a **Mad** magazine, and without **Mad** there would never have been any iconoclastic underground comics in the '60s." That's true, and that's about the best thing we can say for Tijuana Bibles: They are the missing link in American comic satire. They connect the amorous mis-adventures of Obadiah Oldbuck to Harvey Kurtzman's **Mad**, and because **Mad** influenced every single postwar American cartoonist, the Tijuana Bibles are the primordial ancestors of our modern alternative, or underground, comic books.

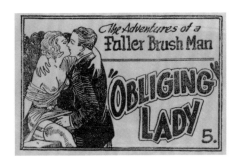

THE BEAST

jack t. chick

In 1961 a different kind of countercultural comic book made its appearance in the United States. These comics were written and drawn by a cartoonist known only as J.T.C., whose fans formed a worldwide underground distribution network dedicated to leaving millions and millions of his little pocket-sized comic books in public where anyone could find them and keep them. J.T.C. was Jack T. Chick, a Los Angeles cartoonist who grew up as a self-described rebellious youth in the 1930s, during the peak of the Tijuana Bible's popularity. It's safe to assume Chick saw at least some of these comics, because when he began making his own comic books they were strikingly similar to the Bibles.

Like Tijuana Bibles, these little comics were designed to fit in the palm of your hand or your vest pocket. And, like the Tijuana Bibles, they were loaded with stereotypes and aimed primarily at the youth of the lower classes. Similar to the better-known comix about to come into existence, Chick's comics contained way-out, wild depictions of drug use. Nor did they blink at portraying the sexual revolution, including homosexuality, lesbianism, even pedophilia. But they didn't stop at those taboos; they also delved into the supernatural. The stories graphically depicted occult rituals, witchcraft, torture, and even cannibalism. More than anything, they were obsessed with the practice of blood sacrifice, which they depicted in all its forms, but especially the one particular act of blood sacrifice performed by the Romans upon Jesus Christ. The whole point of these comics was to convince you that this one act of sacrifice was without question the most important event in the history of the universe. By substituting the blood of a firstborn child, or the blood of a lamb, with the blood of God, this sacrifice had effectively paid for all of your sins.

Jack T. Chick, creator,
The Beast.
Comic book cover
(Chick Publications)
1988

Jack T. Chick, creator,
Fred Carter, artist,
The Gay Blade.
Comic book panel
(Chick Publications)
1972

Jack T. Chick, creator,
Bewitched?
German edition.
Comic book cover
(Chick Publications)
1972

Jack T. Chick, creator,
Fred Carter, artist,
Soul Story.
Comic book cover
(Chick Publications)
1977

Jack T. Chick, creator,
Fred Carter, artist,
Bad Bob!
Comic book cover
(Chick Publications)
1983

WHO IS IT?

KNOCK KNOCK

IT'S SOFIA, LET ME IN!

TIM, DARLING-- I'M LONELY!

SOFIA, I WANT TO TALK TO YOU!

I'LL SHOW YOU HOW YOU CAN *NEVER* BE LONELY AGAIN!

START THE CAMERAS!

NEXT DAY

LET ME SEE THE FILM!

YOU WON'T BE HAPPY, COLONEL!

FOR GOD SO LOVED THE WORLD, THAT HE GAVE HIS ONLY BEGOTTEN SON THAT WHOSOEVER BELIEVETH IN HIM SHOULD NOT PERISH BUT HAVE EVER- LASTING LIFE.

JOHN 3:16

OH, GOD, FORGIVE MY SINS AND SAVE ME FOR CHRIST'S SAKE, COME INTO MY HEART, LORD JESUS!

YAAAAAH!

SHE BECAME A CHRISTIAN!

NOT ONLY THAT, COLONEL (GULP) SO DID THE CAMERAMAN.

@!!✱✶!!!

I CAN'T BELIEVE IT!--I *FAILED!*

GOODBYE, GOD BLESS YOU BOTH --I'M READY TO LAY DOWN MY LIFE FOR JESUS!

WE'RE PRAYING FOR YOU, SOFIA, WE'LL SEE YOU IN HEAVEN.

THERE SHE IS!-- GRAB HER!

DEAR LORD, THANK YOU FOR SENDING TIMOTHY AND JIM TO TELL ME ABOUT YOUR LOVE AND FOR THE BEAUTIFUL FUTURE YOU HAVE PLANNED FOR ME.

SOFIA! GET BACK TO YOUR CELL!

THE END OF OPERATION BUCHAREST

Not only that, but it could give you unlimited power and eternal life, with one catch: You had to act NOW. It was literally a once-in-a-lifetime offer. And if you didn't accept this offer, the comics made it perfectly clear where you were going.

Chick has made close to one hundred books by now, and certain patterns keep repeating. **The Visitors** begins with two young, husky Bible-beaters who go door to door for God, paying a visit to a lonely, middle-aged widow who lets them in and submits herself to their authority. **The Thief** begins with a masked cat burglar entering a bedroom in the middle of the night and startling the occupant, who — surprise, surprise — welcomes the sinner with open arms. **Wounded Children** is about a bearded man in a turtleneck who visits gay bars to tell the guys that he knows of a special love they've never felt before. Then there's the patient in the hospital whose nurse slips in after the others have gone to sleep to tell him that she loves him; the attractive schoolmistress who throws a slumber party for her teenage girls; and so on. In almost all of Chick's religious conversion fantasies, strangers meet and, through a combination of wooden dialogue, bad acting, and bad editing, immediately establish an unrealistic level of intimacy, followed by a lot of gasping, sobbing, and at least one person on his or her knees, ending with a close-up of tears rolling down the submissive one's cheeks. These pornographic conventions make Chick's tracts the Tijuana Bibles of Christianity, and they have proven extremely popular. In the past forty years, Chick has blanketed the earth with over 500 million copies of his books in over one hundred languages. His office in Southern California employs thirty-five people and in 2001 took in over $3 million in sales.

Jack T. Chick, creator,
Fred Carter, artist,
Operation Bucharest,
Crusader's Comic, vol. I.
Comic book panel
(Chick Publications)
1974

today's underground comics

Self-publishing remains the root of most underground comics, even for the comics and cartoonists who are at last making inroads into more traditional bookstores. After Art Spiegelman's **Maus**, Chris Ware's **Jimmy Corrigan, The Smartest Kid on Earth** is probably the most well known and emblematic of the new, post-1970s underground comic books. Like the work of Töpffer, the Tijuana Bible artists, and Chick, **Jimmy Corrigan** began its life as a small, rectangular, self-published booklet that Ware peddled himself at a few independent shops in Chicago and elsewhere. By the time Ware finished his book, ten years and some 360 pages later, it was published between hard covers by Pantheon Books and won the **Guardian** newspaper's First Book award — making it the first comic book to compete on an even playing field with literary fiction and win. So it would seem that underground comics are finally poised to break out of their ghetto. However, comic books in the traditional comic format, i.e.,

the booklet or pamphlet format, face a formidable obstacle, namely what is called the "direct market." Because underground comic books are now rarely, if ever, sold in head shops and the like, they are confined by this "direct market" to the superhero comic shops it serves, and superhero comic shops are the worst place to sell anything other than superhero comics. Yet this is the very market that Ware's **Acme Novelty Library**, his series of irregular comic booklets, is restricted to. For years **Acme** sold around twenty thousand copies per issue through this market, making it a runaway smash hit by alternative comic standards, yet this is still only half of what a run-of-the-mill '70s underground comic sold. Perhaps the publishers of underground comics should court not only literary bookstores but also head shops and porn shops, to get back to the world of sex and drugs from which they came. After all, more average Americans smoke pot and buy vibrators than read **Aquaman**. ✳

works consulted

My condensation of Patrick Rosenkranz's attempt to pinpoint the origin of an underground comix movement is taken from his book *Rebel Visions: The Underground Comix Revolution, 1963–1975* (Seattle: Fantagraphics Books, 2002).

My discussion of Rodolphe Töpffer is a composite drawn from several sources, mainly "Töpffer in America," by Doug Wheeler, Robert L Beerbohm, and Leonardo De Sá, *Comic Art*, no. 3 (Summer 2003): 28–47; as well as E. Wiese (ed., trans.), *Enter: The Comics. Rodolphe Töpffer's Essay on Physiognomy and the True Story of Monsieur Crépin* (University of Nebraska Press, 1965); David Kunzle, *History of the Comic Strip,* vol. 2, *The Nineteenth Century* (Berkeley: University of California Press, c. 1990); and John Oxenford (trans.), *Conversations of Goethe with Eckermann and Soret* (1875).

My discussion of the Tijuana Bibles is drawn from Bob Adelman, *Tijuana Bibles: Art and Wit in America's Forbidden Funnies, 1930s–1950s* (Simon and Schuster, 1997), including the introduction by Art Spiegelman and the commentary by Richard Merkin. My take on Jack Chick is drawn from my own self-published booklet about Chick, *The Imp #2: The Holy War of Jack T. Chick* (1998) and from Robert Ito's article, "Fear Factor," which appeared in *Los Angeles* magazine (May 2003): 56–63.

Jaime Hernandez's "Locas"

Todd Hignite

While the current flowering of North American art comics owes an undeniable debt to the pioneering and liberating work of the late-1960s underground comix movement, the specific sources of most of today's work began to take shape in the early- to mid-1980s "alternative" period. These predominantly black-and-white comics, published independently from the two major mainstream American companies, were distinctive in terms of subject matter, narrative strategies, and method of distribution, representing a middle ground between the heyday of the underground and the widespread critical and commercial attention paid to today's work, which has now been completely freed from any genre restrictions or commercially dictated editorial control and is marked by unrivalled formal invention and conceptual sophistication.

One of the most important cartoonists to emerge from the alternative period is Jaime Hernandez, whose ongoing serialized "Locas" stories published in *Love and Rockets*, which he has continued to expand, deepen, and inter-weave, demonstrate unparalleled character development and highly nuanced emotional resonance in the medium.[1] Built as much on the classical mid-century American tradition of comic book cartooning as informed by the revolutionary taboo breaking of the '60s underground artists, Hernandez's work encompasses many of the formal and narrative concerns (self-reflexive examination of earlier modes of cartooning, and the depiction of marginalized subcultures—for Hernandez, the Mexican-American culture of Southern California and the early and gradually fading punk rock milieu) of the two generations. As such, while acting as a bridge between the underground and now, his ever-evolving tapestry, poignantly chronicling the human condition with unparalleled candor and affection (his true subject matter), has gone far in paving the way for myriad contemporary approaches to the art form.[2]

Jaime Hernandez,
"Mechanics: Part Two,"
Love and Rockets #7,
page 6.
Comic book panel
(Fantagraphics Books)
1984

Jaime Hernandez,
Love and Rockets #1.
Comic book cover
(Fantagraphics Books)
1982

Jaime Hernandez,
Love and Rockets #24.
Comic book cover
(Fantagraphics Books)
1987

Jaime Hernandez,
Love and Rockets #15.
Comic book cover
(Fantagraphics Books)
1986

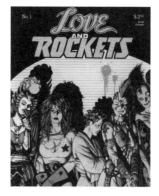

love & rockets

Created along with his brothers Mario and Gilbert, **Love and Rockets**, first self-published in 1981 with an expanded version released by Fantagraphics Books in 1982, marked a pivotal point in the burgeoning alternative movement. Young cartoonists working during this time were armed with an expansive history at their disposal, covering both commercial genre comic books of their youth and newly reprinted historical comic strips, as well as the mind-bending (and taboo-decimating) undergrounds. In fact, Hernandez's clean approach — influenced by comic book artists from adventure and superhero maestros Alex Toth and Steve Ditko to humorists Owen Fitzgerald and Dan DeCarlo — can be viewed in contrast to the more ornate homegrown styles favored by the underground cartoonists (think no-frills punk rock versus hippie psychedelia); his style and subject matter reference artistic predecessors, but always with an idiosyncratic twist. The reliance on traditional genres is clear in the early work of both Jaime and Gilbert, but from the outset is marked by an unmistakable personal interpretation of past conventions, always tweaked by the brothers' aesthetic rooted in topical real-life human drama, and only explicitly for the first handful of issues, subsequently recurring through their more finely honed sensibilities as subtle nods. The time

period that gave rise to **Love and Rockets** then can be seen as "in-between," in that personal, artistic-minded work employed numerous genre trappings, albeit in a recombined and increasingly removed and ironic manner. As the undergrounds demonstrated, comics are an inherently self-reflexive medium, so for an artist as immersed in the form as Hernandez, any and all commercial and artistic genres — romance, science-fiction, superhero, "real-life" character types (the underground bohemian lifestyle merely an additional genre) — are elements (fictional, in a sense) to be combined, exploited, and transcended all at once, reconfigured in the unique language of comics to create expansive, poetic inner reality.[3]

While such references informed his underlying sensibility, Hernandez's groundbreakingly "realistic" depiction of everyday lives, focusing to a large degree on women and minorities, is his most impressive achievement, and the aspect most critically commented upon. However, it is not the mere inclusion of a particular subject matter, rather *how* the artist treats the material in comic form that is revolutionary, and Hernandez perfectly fuses his content and the form in never less than surprising ways.

LOVE AND ROCKETS

No. 15 ■ $2.25
$3.15 in Canada

RENA

JAIME 84

FANTAGRAPHICS BOOKS

A close examination of a dizzyingly rich single page from the middle of his "Locas" installments, which touches on nearly all of the formal and narrative elements from his stories over the last twenty-five years, provides great insight into the artist's virtuosity. The page — taken from Hernandez's novel-length and arguably most impressive self-contained story to date, "Wigwam Bam," a panoramic meditation on absence (which also delves into ethnic and provincial stereotypes) collected into book form in 1994 from its early 1990s serialization within the pages of **Love and Rockets** — is dominated by a single horizontal panel, which, at once chaotic and sharply composed, overwhelms the space. The first panel depicts a flashback experienced by Hopey, one of the primary characters in the story, triggered by a conversation with Maggie, Hernandez's main protagonist over the years. The artist fades into the flashback by gradually draining the second panel of background detail, focusing exclusively on the two characters and their immediately evident relationship in the foreground. As Hopey physically turns from Maggie in the second panel, the narrative also pivots away from the temporal and physical space leading up to the exchange.[4] Riot-gear-clad Los Angeles policemen replace the hallway of an East Coast apartment building. The shift is abruptly completed in the large center panel, the background emptiness replaced by a swarming mass of punk rockers taunting and facing off against the police; stark white is replaced by seething black. The police themselves do not appear again in this page; only their introduction in the second panel alerts the viewer to their presence, and thus the context of the flashback.

The transition is simultaneously decisive and gradual: both places and times are linked by the urban background, introduced in the first panel as an anonymous East Coast cityscape in the distance seen through a window, then Los Angeles. The fourth panel elaborates the scene, introducing other supporting characters. In the fifth, the significantly younger Hopey and Maggie, along with a friend, playfully sing as the aforementioned crowd surges toward impending confrontation. Contrasts abound in the page, yet visual and textual links bridge time and space. In no other medium could these scenes be interspersed and produced to the same effect; in no other medium could the reader/viewer experience the same collision of time and locale, emotional involvement, and formal and conceptual flow.

Hernandez foregoes superficial formal experimentation in order to concentrate on the narrative: his layout is exactly symmetrical and the focus is within the panels rather than on the structure of the panels themselves (which relies on a traditional comic book grid of three tiers, each composed of one, two or three panels), and variation of form is always rejected in favor of narrative progression. Deceptively simple black-and-white lines define space and weight. Extreme backgrounds are predominantly solid black or white, foregrounding the emphasis on the individual characters and their interactions (or lack thereof); this focus on visceral emotional involvement is reflected in the formal arrangement, which lands the reader squarely in the middle of the action. While it may not be immediately evident, the adherence to such a repetitive format is as conceptually reflective and formally tied to the emotional underpinnings of the narrative as overt design and layout experimentation, merely more understated, as the reader is effectively integrated directly into the narrative; every element is considered — even the hand-rendered quality of the panel borders ushers forth the overall tone. In both cases, the formal language painstakingly paints the emotional backdrop for the projected worldview, and in Hernandez's work the format is subsumed by the continual flow of the story; while finely crafted images serve numerous purposes simultaneously, there are no hard melodramatic breaks. It goes on and on. The structure is intentionally repetitious, without splashiness, only slight variation, always inexorably moving forward — toward life's uncertain future.

Jaime Hernandez,
"Wigwam Bam,"
Love and Rockets
#33, page 8.
Comic book panel
(Fantagraphics Books)
1990

Jaime Hernandez,
"Locas Tambien,"
Love and Rockets #4,
page 1.
Comic book panel
(Fantagraphics Books)
1983

VIDA LOCA 2

The sprawling middle panel is a contemporary frieze frozen in time. The smaller surrounding panels incorporate word balloons, providing interaction, while the center panel is entirely devoid of text—language—reduced to pure image. The figures are spot-lit, an effect that heightens the inherent iconic stature of the cleanly inked comic image. A single character stands apart from the crowd, pushed even further forward in the picture plane, his scale punctuating the band of figures behind him. Despite the cramped inclusion of at least nineteen clearly delineated figures, the image is static, and the potential rioters do not interact, rather react simultaneously to the off-page presence of the police mass. As in the most successful comics, temporality is halted in a manner not possible in any other medium, not in isolation but in both narrative and "real" time. The visual language of cartooning always serves at least a dual purpose: static expressions and gestures are framed and rendered iconic, and each, expertly composed, lurches the eye to a halt even as it is led, faster or slower, through the narrative, paced by the empty gaps between panels, the implication of the before and after always lurking. Here the gaze of every figure strikes directly out at the viewer, activating the scene. Space is flattened and pushed forward to the extreme of the panel surface; the viewer is thrust into the foreground while the shallow diorama foregrounds the artifice of the drawn symbols. In the face of the implied police threat, expressions range from arrogant, antagonistic, and fearful to bemused and disinterested, a diverse gamut that serves as metaphor for both the reaction of the depicted subculture to pinning down (by art), and of the comic language to superficial prejudice.

Hernandez is able to tell extremely complex stories through details and the unique combination of the visual and textual properties of the language. There is an inherently fetishistic quality to the form, and the always carefully rendered minutiae in his art, folds of clothing, the gleam of leather, and the slightest hand gesture, blossom into unseen emotional and physical universes. The symbolic truth found in his snappy and increasingly pared down shorthand style, which provides only the vital marks necessary to define characters and hint at unseen narrative offshoots, transcends realism. Notice the hatch line delineating the jeans of the center panel's leading figure, swiftly rendered with a swagger that matches the combative stance of the jeering young man. (Compare this effect to that of Robert Crumb's fuzzed-out droopy inking style for his spiritual-questing hippies, and the conceptual underpinnings of the form are immediately evident.) While the art reads fast and slow simultaneously — fluttering between the traditional commercial prerequisite of moving the story along and the art of forcing the eye to linger on telling/symbolic details — Hernandez's narrative rhythm is never interrupted. He, more than any contemporary cartoonist, has harnessed the ability of a previous generation of craftsmen to delicately exploit the perfectly rendered, slick (seemingly the antithesis of expressive) line to create a world unimaginable in another medium. As the artist states of his aesthetic: "I felt if one line could do the same job as a hundred it would make a far more impressive image. It's like growing older. There are just some silly details in life that don't matter as much as they did when you're younger. I'd like to think my line has matured over the years, for lack of a humbler anecdote."[5] The details that do remain practically vibrate with

emotional intensity, transcending the functional goals of mere illustration.

In "Wigwam Bam," as in all his work, Hernandez movingly weds multi-layered narratives with radical fissures of time, place, and point of view. Entire histories are implied by understated visual cues, triggered by slight marks on paper. Hernandez's command of black-and-white weight, static solidity, and perspective highlights the inherent unreality of the comic language as a blatant distancing device effective at critiquing any action or situation. He creates multi-faceted (i.e., realistic) depictions of women, replete with humor and pathos, always resisting didacticism, within stories that incorporate an instant back-and-forth totality, representing the challenge of the medium: to visually depict the non-visual — thoughts and memory — by using the form's collectively remembered, standardized techniques, incorporating genre clichés in the creation of radically new subject matter and stylistic invention. Unlike many artistic-minded cartoonists, whose protagonists seem thinly veiled stand-ins for the author's viewpoints, Hernandez allows his characters to be contradictory and fully modeled, more and less aware of their environments — he is always warmly accepting, never embarrassed of foible, and never proffers one-dimensional moralizing judgment.

The abrupt switches in locale and compositional density from panel to panel are achieved through harsh black-and-white contrasts that create a disjunctive swirl through positive and negative space. Each panel activates the oscillating psychological space between characters as a physical presence. In his exploitation of such visual and narrative devices, Hernandez draws on and experiments with the medium's intertextual past. The use of a slick "cartoony" approach references a history of seemingly innocuous strips

Jaime Hernandez,
"Jerusalem Crickets,"
Love and Rockets #21,
page 2.
Comic book panel
(Fantagraphics Books)
1987

Jaime Hernandez,
Love and Rockets #5.
Comic book cover
(Fantagraphics Books)
1984

focusing on cute children in quaint situations (specifically Charles Schulz's **Peanuts** and **Dennis the Menace** by Hank Ketcham). However, here the codified, reductive line work is injected with narrative elements that have no direct precedent in the medium. By drawing the reader in with an immediately recognizable short-hand cartooning style, Hernandez is able to create a shock of awareness that ciphers greater emotional involvement in the narrative. Crucially, his clean style is used as a means for the reader to easily inhabit an unfamiliar world (a juxtaposition that can be likened to Art Spiegelman's use of cartoon animals in his Holocaust survival tale **Maus**). If the

art was superficially expressive it would overwhelm, and the message would be lost.[6] Hernandez's devotion to expressing such a personal vision in the realm of comics is more striking and impressive when taking into consideration his widely acclaimed graphic talent. No matter the specifics of the narrative, the gracefulness of Hernandez's art conveys the perpetual warmth of humanity under-lying all situations.

His is pure cartooning where meaning lies firmly in the combination of textual details and the overall narrative rhythm — the in-between — where abstraction and figuration are perfectly merged. Of critical impor-tance is Hernandez's aforementioned

ability to consistently massage the medium to function on numerous levels simultaneously.[7] The cool artifice of the shorthand language never purports to be "reality," rather it is always partially empty, allowing for interpretive embellishment between the panels, and is ripe for explorations into the symbolic function of the form's pictorial artificiality. In drawing on this constant in-between quality, self-reflexive nature, and the medium's nebulous cultural position, the most successful contemporary work is always effective as metaphor. So form is always content, and vice versa.[8]

The recurring underlying subtext of Hernandez's work for the last decade — building since virtually the outset — has been the reconciliation of youthful idealism and blind faith with the hum-drum world of workaday normalcy. Crucially, Hernandez continues to tell stories after their superficial appeal has passed, detailing lives once the excitement of youth and all that goes along with it fades to memory. How much of life after a given period is made up of remembrances, reactions to that time? The seeming formlessness or lack of firm narrative direction in later "Locas" stories is exactly the point. While richly engaging, as only the most complex art can be, Hernandez's all-encompassing stories are also endlessly entertaining, altering one's perception of the world while the full range of humanity dances on and below the surface of the page; in other words, all of his formal virtuosity and refinement is in the service of characterization. The focus is always on lives writ, on the characters to whom he returns as they age over time. Hernandez's evolving dramas, which have become deeply ingrained by nature of the installments' serial form, set his work apart; the reader is perpetually looking forward to the future. Characters are followed forward and backward in time, always there for the reader to return to — this is how they remain alive. The primary reward of a prolonged immersion in Hernandez's ongoing world is the continued resonance of his intricately rendered landscape. For all the discussion of "realism" and well-rounded characters, the potency truly lies in the in-between — in-between perfectly paced "real life" and symbolic fantasy — that makes the emotional reaction all the more heightened (his early superheroes and space princesses — and rockets — can at this point be read as almost purely internalized, wistful metaphors).

Above all, there is an honesty in Hernandez's comics, even when framed in superficially unbelievable situations: this honesty lies in the constantly conflicting emotions and motivations that lead to all manner of heartbreak and self-destruction on the way toward spiritual fulfill-ment. The punk milieu and its aftermath, remembered in its roman-tically idealistic light, is a true, over-saturated, microcosm of such pitfalls. These themes are beautifully articulated, yet it is impossible to reductively pigeonhole Hernandez's ineffable vision — as messy and sometimes contradictory as life itself — which is perfectly realized (if not contained) by his spare, virtuosic art. The much-lauded reality of **Love and Rockets** then does not stem from documentary exactitude (although the accumulation of telling details creates a subliminal piecing together of events into a perfectly integrated world in the mind of the reader), but rather from the combination and juxtaposition of what is depicted and left out, internal monologues, too often humble existence, and dream life. Hernandez, more skillfully than any cartoonist the medium has seen, creates a total reality, much more effective than one-note reportage, from all-encompassing artistic invention. Here "real life" is evinced as the cumulative effect of his ongoing anticlimactic rhythm. This achievement is infinitely more realistic than "realism," as it accentuates the fantastic and ever-shifting internal impressionism of the human experience.

The strengths of Hernandez's work are the strengths of the best contemporary achievements within the current golden age of the medium, which continually occupies a shimmeringly multivalent, in-between state. Comic art's unique characteristics position the medium as the permanent interloper, always nimbly straddling a nebulous status between high and low, writing and drawing, and literature and art, that has proved resistant to definition and led to the form's perpetual misreading. Cartoonists exploit expected genre conventions as allegory and cultural critique, in order to achieve a visual poetry, a universal truth, the implication of the general (larger themes) through the depiction of the specific. Such volatility provides a formal and narrative spark for the medium.[9] A key to understanding Hernandez's work is the manner in which it epitomizes how inherently self-reflexive comic books have become. The lack of firm categor-ization is reflected in his subject matter, content, and artistic approach — characters in-between youthful idealism and adulthood — and is a defining characteristic of work stemming from the alternative movement of the 1980s. In the hands of Jaime Hernandez, then, the medium has become an amazingly conceptual language, wherein an entire history, a shared past, is referenced in a single brush stroke or pen flourish. But while Hernandez's work is symbolic of artistic advances that began in the '80s and continue to blossom today, he stands alone in his creation and continued exploration of a profound, fully realized cast of emotionally inhabitable locales and lives, articulated with unerring poetic precision and warmth. ✴

1 The first incarnation of *Love and Rockets* was a magazine format comic, published from 1982 to 1996 by Fantagraphics Books. After taking a five-year break from the title and creating separate comic books, Jaime and his brother Gilbert Hernandez returned to *Love and Rockets* as a comic-book-sized comic in 2001, with the same content format as the original magazine: individual work by Jaime and Gilbert, with occasional contributions from older brother Mario.

2 During the 1980s a number of factors made it possible for artists to create comics outside of the work-for-hire system used by the two major publishers, Marvel and DC. The direct market system of distribution and the related proliferation of specialty comic shops enabled a market to develop outside of the traditional mainstream venues of the past; an alternative framework for disseminating comic books had become prevalent by the early 1970s as a means for the undergrounds to flourish. More obviously important than developing new venues for comics, underground creators demolished content restriction, radically altering standard genre domination. For an in-depth discussion of the relationship between underground and alternative comics in form, content, and distribution, see the first chapter of Charles Hatfield's forthcoming book *Alternative Comics: An Emerging Literature* (working title), set for publication in spring 2005 by the University Press of Mississippi.

3 If on one level Hernandez's virtuosity can be seen as a combination of American mainstream cartooning traditions and the liberties of underground subject matter (although notably without the over-the-top shock value; Hernandez is always subtle, even when overt), it is important to note that underground cartoonists performed similar deconstructions of past comic influences by isolating formal and textual elements and exploding genre conventions, and that such self-awareness was in turn strongly influenced by the cultural critiques of the Harvey Kurtzman–edited *Mad* from the mid-1950s – truly a touchstone for virtually everything that followed.

4 This is merely one example of Hernandez's mastery and the constant polyphony in his work, which harmoniously juxtaposes two or more simultaneous narrative threads, be they visual, verbal, or both (a quality inherent to the comic language).

5 Jaime Hernandez, email correspondence with the author, 27 September 2001.

6 Regarding his stylistic approach, Hernandez has stated, "I want the presentation to be as clear as possible. I didn't want to fool anybody.... I wasn't trying to make a fool of anybody, I wasn't trying to dazzle them with my new groundbreaking work... It was pretty much 'These stories, this world, these people are interesting enough where they don't need help, they don't need any help from stylizing or anything like that.'" Jaime Hernandez, interview by Chris Knowles, *Comic Book Artist*, no. 15 (November 2001): 58.

7 In the work of contemporary cartoonists, the historical cultural status of the comic form can be frequently read as a subtext within the narrative. Depending on subject matter and audience, a strategic shifting positionality is used in order to critique various high and low stereotypes. Due to the perpetual marginalization of the medium by the fine art world, what are seen to be the pretensions of high art are frequently attacked through cagey reveling in the stereotypical low, or outsider, subculture. In this page, the perceived reception of the form by the art world may be read as an implied commentary by the subject matter itself: the misunderstood, exploited, and co-opted culture of punk rock. The mohawked figure in the right corner of the center panel exemplifies this stance, symbolically mocking interpretive attempts as he literally mocks the attempted control by the police. In addition to a rejection of stratified high cultural values, sophisticated cartoonists often express disdain at the continuing superhero tradition, presenting this slowly dying form as low "trash" in comparison to more personal and subjective subject matter, thus adopting an aestheticized stance versus more standardized aspects of popular culture. Hernandez demonstrates how contemporary cartoonists employ the status of the medium as a critical, self-reflexive tour de force, perpetually floating between high and low, enabling a critique of both.

8   While such a close reading of individual panels within a single page taken from a lengthy narrative provides an introduction to understanding the formal richness of the medium, it is done with an awareness of the limitations of divorcing an individual page as singular art object from its larger context. Such analysis alone is an interpretive mistake in reading that constantly occurs in art world discussion of the comic form, an approach that presupposes a vocabulary already in existence within the theoretical framework of art history. What such discussion fails to take into account is the unique position, aesthetically and culturally, of the historical comic book and strip, and how the contemporary comic book draws on such a history in order to create a unique language begging for alternative theorization. The confused search for the medium's "art" in single panel, page, or entire story is reflected in the confused reception of individual artistic achievement within a "mass" form. Hernandez's opus must be read in its entirety to be fully appreciated.

9   Hernandez's description of his primary ongoing character again reinforces the fact that cartoonists are intimately aware of this history—and internalize it as an inherent element of the language, mirrored occasionally in the narrative itself: "Maggie is told 'You're a great mechanic', and she thinks, 'Oh, OK'. She has that guilt of being a girl mechanic when she wasn't supposed to be; when she should have been dating boys. It's her Mexican upbringing that she just can't shake. She's learned to be a good Mexican. When she's a Mexican-American, she's kind of caught between being a good Mexican and a good American. I take that from my upbringing: You're caught in the middle, and you can't please either side. So she feels like a failure, even though she's very intelligent and very talented at what *she used to do*. But she just has this block that doesn't let her get anywhere." Jaime Hernandez, interview by Amy Benfer, 20 February 2001. "Los Bros Hernandez duet, with kissing," on Salon.com.

59

The 1960s, African Americans,
and the
American
Comic Book

Gerald Early

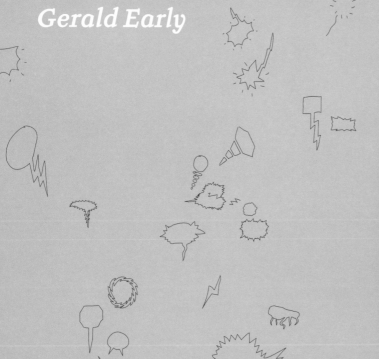
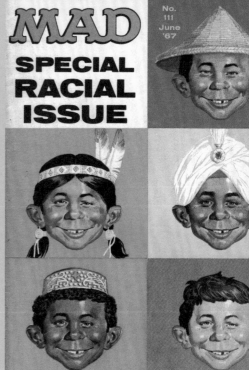

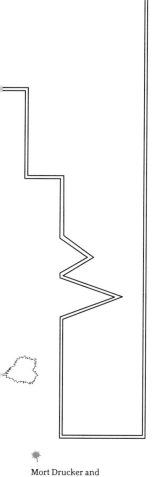

Mort Drucker and
Larry Siegel,
Mad "Special Racial
Issue" #III.
Comic book cover
(Mad, EC Publications)
June 1967

In June 1967, *Mad* magazine published a "Special Racial Issue," which featured multiple Alfred E. Newmans on the cover as a Native American, a South Asian Indian, a Chinese, an African, and a Caucasian. The lead parody in that issue was entitled "Stokely and Tess," what the magazine called "A Modern *Mad* Version of 'Porgy and Bess.'" The parody was about the conflict within the civil rights movement between Martin Luther King, Jr., the head of the Southern Christian Leadership Conference (SCLC), Nobel Laureate, and certainly the most noted and popular black leader of the 1960s, and his advocacy of nonviolence, and Stokely Carmichael, the chairman of the Student Nonviolent Coordinating Committee (SNCC), veteran of voter registration drives in Alabama, and the advocate, indeed the popularizer, of the slogan Black Power. Mort Drucker, *Mad*'s best caricaturist, and Larry Siegel, a writer who became known for his bitingly controversial *Mad* send-ups of television shows like *Hogan's Heroes*, in which he tried to show "the idiocy of a program which would have fun with a time when there was such horror going on and make it seem so light,"[1] combined to do the satire. A subject like the civil rights movement, clearly so pervasive in American society at the time that it virtually achieved pop-culture status—its leaders among the most written about and publicized black people in America—would seem a bit dangerous to tackle, the politics of the moment being so tensely drawn and the subject appearing on its surface not to lend itself well to any sort of humor.[2] That is to say, it would seem that the subject offered too many booby-traps, too many ways for a humorous treatment of it to backfire. Television shows and movies seemed a safer bet than satirizing a political movement and particularly satirizing race as a political and social concept in America. But as Siegel himself said, "If you're afraid, then forget the satire business. I think anything is fair game if you do it right."[3] Was "Stokely and Tess" done right and according to whom?

Curiously, Drucker and Siegel decided to use *Porgy and Bess* as the vehicle for their satire. They mention in their headnote to "Stokely and Tess" that there "has been talk lately that 'Porgy and Bess' may be brought back to Broadway." It would have been unlikely that the opera would have returned to Broadway in the late 1960s, considering the mood of the country, and especially the mood of black people, some of whom probably would have vigorously protested such a revival. Otto Preminger directed and Samuel Goldwyn produced the film version in 1959, probably the most expensive film with an all-black cast ever made to that point, with a set alone that cost $2 million[4] (and possibly still the most expensive all-black-cast movie now, if the costs are adjusted to today's dollars). The film caused a great deal of consternation and despair in the black artistic community. Neither Dorothy Dandridge nor Sidney Poitier, the two leads, wanted to do the film as they both felt the opera was dated and full of offensive stereotypes of black life, as well as offensive dialect. Harry Belafonte, who had starred four years earlier with Dorothy Dandridge in the Preminger-directed musical *Carmen Jones*, and who was rumored to be the top candidate for the lead, flatly refused to a play a role on his knees portraying a lowlife character.[5] It was the new age of integration and political activism among blacks and *Porgy and Bess* was simply no longer an acceptable vehicle. Pearl Bailey, another important actor in the film, was wary as well.[6] Many blacks voiced strong disapproval of filming the opera for the same reason—it suggested that blacks were lowlife people with "folksy" poignancy— although many approved of, or at least acquiesced to, the idea that the project would employ a number of black actors and provide them a showcase for their talents, largely the same feeling that many blacks had

about the opera when it premiered in 1935. African Americans' relationship to *Porgy and Bess* has always been curious and complicated. (Duke Ellington never liked the opera, thinking it inauthentic in its depiction of black life and in its use of black musical idioms, although it was "grand music and a swell play."[7]) If the average reader of *Mad* was, at that time, a teenager between, say, twelve and eighteen, then the film *Porgy and Bess* was certainly released within the lifetime and memory of *Mad*'s readers, although it would not likely have been a film that their readers would have liked or even have seen. Yet Drucker and Siegel thought the opera was so familiar that its arias, many of them popular songs in the Great American Songbook, would be known by its young audience and could be effectively parodied. The fact that the 1959 film version sparked a spate of popular *Porgy and Bess* recordings including the Gil Evans/Miles Davis legendary album, Oscar Peterson's trio recording, the Louis Armstrong/ Ella Fitzgerald version, the Lena Horne/Harry Belafonte version,[8] the remarkable R-and-B rendition of "Summertime" by Billy Stewart, and Nina Simone's poignant signature reading of "I Loves You, Porgy" may also have helped spread the familiarity of the opera. How much that young, overwhelmingly white audience may have felt that *Mad* was poking fun at the conflicts of the civil rights movement and black people through, above anything contained in the actual parody, its choice of the vehicle with which to satirize it, is open to question. Certainly, many of the young blacks involved in SNCC and the civil rights movement who doubtless remembered the movie and who probably saw the *Mad* satire were, it is safe to say, not amused. To link the drama of the movement to the plot and music of *Porgy and Bess* had to be insulting. The fact that the

mad magazine

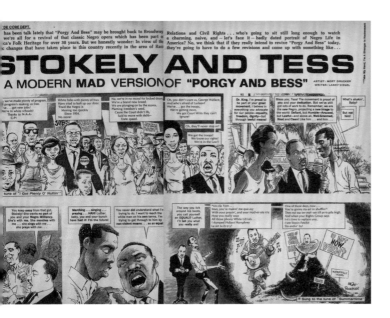

Mort Drucker and
Larry Siegel,
Mad "Special Racial
Issue" #III, pages 4–5.
Comic book panel
(Mad, EC Publications)
June 1967

© 1967 EC Publications, Inc.
All rights reserved. Used with
permission.

Mad satirists were Jewish was probably not lost on some blacks, who felt that Drucker and Siegel were defining black experience just as George and Ira Gershwin did in writing the opera. As blacks grew more militant in the 1960s, the tension between them and Jews grew.

But it is the linkage of the civil rights movement to popular culture through **Porgy and Bess** and through the mix of political characters—King and Carmichael—with pop culture stars like Muhammad Ali, Sammy Davis, Jr., and Dick Gregory that made "Stokely and Tess" so incisive, because the satire teetered at poking fun at what the movement was becoming through poking fun at what the movement was trying to over- come and defeat: Negroes as a set of inauthentic, histrionic poses of themselves trying to express a political notion of what it means to be a Negro. Yet the satire in no way trades on comic stereotypes or insulting images of blacks as primitives or simpletons. The civil rights movement had become something of a self-conscious performance, something of a self- conscious mythology, deeply American in the sources it made reference to and deeply American as a source of cultural expression, and the satire reflects this complexity. "Stokely and Tess" was a turning point

in the depiction of blacks in American comics; for the satire itself was an odd form of homage saying that African Americans and the political nature of their struggle had become so critical in understanding American life itself, and so familiar to American life, that they and the civil rights movement needed to be taken seriously in humor in a way that was quite distinct from the ways that blacks had been the subject of American humor in the past. Blacks, in the satire, were funny not because they were presented as a sort of fantasy or a projection of the white mind but because of the contradictory nature of their aspirations as Americans. "Stokely and Tess" was, in fact, a profound piece of humor.

The *Mad* satire was published exactly one year after Black Power became the new slogan in the tangled, violent, unsettled world of American racial politics of the 1960s, which saw a shift from the integrationist, non-violent tactics of King's SCLC-led marches to violent urban riots such as the 1965 Watts riot. The growing opposition to the escalating war in Vietnam intensified a sense of nationalistic militancy among African Americans. The shift was captured most dramatically with the change in leadership of SNCC, when in May 1966 John Lewis was voted out as chairman in favor of

the more radically militant Stokely Carmichael. It was at a rally on June 16, 1966, in Greenwood, Mississippi, that Carmichael uttered the phrase "Black Power!"

The fact that one year later **Mad** was able to parody this split showed how deeply Black Power, which had become a byword in American racial politics only one year earlier, had penetrated the American mind, so deeply that Drucker and Siegel assumed their readers understood the basic nature of the conflict. After all, a parody or satire can work only if someone is familiar with the issues and personalities being targeted. Never before in American history had black political aspirations and goals been so widely known and such a subject of not simply debate but of cultural expression. Not even during slavery were the inner workings of **black** political organization and the complexities of **black** political thought such a vibrant source of interest in the culture. The **Mad** magazine satire of the civil rights movement and Black Power was part of a larger trend in the 1960s that depicted blacks in comics in a far different way than they had generally been depicted before.

Stan Lee, script,
Jack Kirby, art,
Joe Sinnott, inks,
Artie Simek, lettering,
Fantastic Four #52.
Comic book cover
(Marvel Comics)
July 1966

Stan Lee, script,
Jack Kirby, art,
Joe Sinnott, inks,
Artie Simek, lettering,
Fantastic Four #53.
Comic book cover
(Marvel Comics)
August 1966

fantastic four

The July and August 1966 issues of Marvel Comics' popular title the **Fantastic Four** (#52 and #53) introduced the first costumed black superhero, T'Challa, the Black Panther. Marvel writer Stan Lee and artist Jack Kirby, who invented the character,[9] could not have been influenced by the famed Black Panther Party of Oakland, California, which did not adopt the symbol of the black panther or formulate its program until the fall of 1966 and did not formally become an organization until early 1967. It is also unlikely that either Kirby or Lee had even heard of the Lowndes County, Alabama, Freedom Organization that was formed by SNCC and the black people of that area in 1965 and which became known as the Black Panther Party, the inspiration for the more famous Oakland, California, organization.[10] Both Kirby and Lee simply drew the name from the jungle comic tradition, which they were both amply familiar with, considering their long involvement in creating comics. (The name of Black Panther might have been partly suggested by Princess Pantha, a famous white jungle queen of the 1940s and 1950s who appeared in **Thrilling Comics**.) What Kirby and Lee had done, with the creation of this black superhero, was give comic book readers a twist on two conventions, two fantasies of comics, which, in fact, were two conventions of the pulp literature that inspired comics: primitive blacks in the African jungle and the selfless, violent, white superhero as righteous vigilante. They tried, in response to the politics of the 1960s, to redeem these two racist ideas that were part of the major creative backbone of modern comics, of pulp culture.

W. Morgan Thomas,
Jumbo Comics #75.
Comic book cover
(Real Adventures
Publication Co.)
May 1945

Jungle comics were a popular genre in the 1940s and 1950s particularly, although variants of them still exist today, such as Avatar Comics' ***Jungle Fantasy*** and Dark Horse Comics' first issue of ***Bettie Page Comics*** published in 1996 with a scantily clad Page on the cover looking as if she is about to be ravished by savage African tribesmen. Although Tarzan, the jungle lord, was and remains an archetypical character in American popular culture, and certainly was a major presence in comics, with a good number of knock-offs, most successful jungle comics had femmes fatales as the main characters: jungle queens such as Tiger Girl, Camille, Rulah, Jungle Lil, Lorna, Jann of the Jungle, Nyoka, and the most famous of the lot, Sheena.[11] (Marvel resuscitated Sheena comics as recently as the 1980s and had tried another white jungle queen named Rima the Jungle Girl in the 1970s. Marvel also had their version of Tarzan, a character named Ka-zar.) All of these scantily clad women went around the African jungle (for this topo-graphically diverse continent, in the minds of provincial comic book writers, was nothing more than uncultivated jungle) protecting childish natives from evil whites or from more savage, aggressive tribes who were usually in the thrall of some evil whites. Part of the convention as well was to make sure, either on the cover of the comic or somewhere within its panels, that the jungle queen or some other scantily clad white woman was surrounded by scantily clad African men. There was never any sex or even attempted sex in these comics with a few rare exceptions such as ***Thun'da, King of the Congo*** #2 (one of the many

Tarzan imitations), published in 1952, an even more racist example of the genre than is typically the case, where, in the story called "Cave Girl," drawn by Bob Powell, an African native, who is depicted literally to resemble an ape, tries to kiss a white girl and is promptly killed by an enraged Thun'da, "the white jungle god." The cover of the comic itself is nothing more than a symbolic image of interracial sexual defilement. Of course, these jungle comics were all about titillation, constantly teasing the reader with his own adolescent fantasy about the jungle as a lawless place where interracial sex or, more accurately, interracial rape, may break out at any moment, if it were not for the colonial jungle king or queen reminding the savages that they are, in fact, supposed to be grateful children.[12] (Most of this seems nothing more than lurid allegories about the American race situation, part of which seemed greatly fixated on interracial sex.) As filmmaker D.W. Griffith famously said, "There is nothing, absolutely nothing, calculated to raise the gooseflesh on the back of an audience more than that of a white girl in relation to Negroes."[13]

In introducing the Black Panther, Lee and Kirby give the reader the jungle as a secret repository of science and technology, as it is revealed that the Black Panther is a scientist and engineer who has built a fantastic maze of machinery in the jungle where his tribe serves as his technicians. So, the jungle of the civil rights/Black Power era is not a backward place of savages who need white colonialism, Africans who act like children and have no scientific understanding of the world, but rather a place of technology and

jungle comics

ICTION·ADVENTURE·MYSTERY
JUMBO COMICS
AY
75
10¢
HEENA
JUNGLE QUEEN IN
RROR TRAIL OF THE
EVIL'S HORNS"
HOST GALLERY
Y GIRL·THE HAWK
AND MANY OTHERS

✳
Bob Powell,
*Thun'da King of the
Congo* #2.
Comic book cover
(Magazine Enterprises,
Vincent Sullivan,
Sussex Publishing Co.)
1952

✳
Larry Fuller,
Ebon #1.
Comic book cover
(Spearhead Comics,
San Francisco Comic
Book Co.)
January 1970

advancement disguised as jungle. Kirby and Lee know the conventions they are subverting in doing this. They have the acerbic Thing, one of the members of the Fantastic Four, comment, for instance, in **Fantastic Four** #52, when the group is flying around in one of the Black Panther's inventions: "But how does a refugee from a Tarzan movie lay his hands on this kinda gizmo?" Later, in **Fantastic Four** #53, when the Black Panther tells the Fantastic Four the story of his life, it is the Thing who keeps interrupting with "I saw this in a million jungle movies!" or "I know the rest by heart! Everything wuz hunky dory until the greedy ivory hunters made the scene" or "Yer talkin' to a guy who seen every Tarzan movie at least a dozen times! And I can recite ya half 'a the Bomba the Jungle boy books by heart!" Clearly, Lee and Kirby are using the Thing as a mouthpiece to poke fun not only at the old jungle conventions but also perhaps at the idea of being able to rehabilitate them. The Black Panther's tale does follow some of the pattern of an archetypical jungle story: evil whites do come who wish to exploit the natural minerals of the

place, in this instance, something called vibranium. And the evil white leader, a megalomaniac scientist named Klaw, kills the Black Panther's father, the brave proud chief, T'Chaka. T'Challa, the son, acquires a western education, learns to mine the vibranium for the benefit of himself and his people, and develops his powers as the Black Panther in order to seek revenge against Klaw.

What Lee and Kirby do in combining western technology and the jungle is to idealize Africa as a site where modernity and the primitive meet and co-exist. This polemical, romantic formula was to be used later in black superhero comics such as Spearhead Comics' obscure, clumsily drawn underground comic, **Ebon**, published January 1970, conceived and illustrated by black artist Larry Fuller, where the alien explorer, Jom, who looks like a black man, imparts wisdom to Africans. It is used more compellingly in highly Afrocentric comics like **Zwanna, Son of Zulu** and **Heru, Son of Ausar**, both published in 1993 by ANIA, an independent black company, when the Afrocentrist vision of

ancient Africa as a place of peace, wisdom, and sophisticated high culture, in short an African Eden or African pastoral of a Golden Age, was highly prominent in African American thinking. These books did nothing more than take the Lee and Kirby vision of Africa and, if anything, make it more self-righteously moral in a highly ironical way by insisting that its kitsch-like fiction was something like the unearthing of political and historical truth. **Captain Africa**, another Afrocentrist comic of the 1990s based on some children's books by Dwayne J. Ferguson, is much the same. In trying to create a so-called "positive" mythology about Africa, these efforts actually do not go beyond the mythological and thematic premises of the original Black Panther, which may say something about the series of traps the liberal western mind, both black and white, has fallen into in trying to conceptualize Africa at all. For all of these books, from the **Black Panther** to **Captain Africa**, are about the therapeutic uplift of the African American. They have little enough to do with anything, real or imaginary, connected to the lives of Africans as they live now or ever lived on the continent of Africa.

But the Black Panther was a revolutionary change in how blacks were depicted in comics. And his importance and the range of his influence reside less in how Africa is depicted than in how the character broke the barrier of giving the public a black superhero. When the Black Panther pledges to the Fantastic Four, at their urging, that he will become a superhero—"I pledge my fortune, my powers—my very life—to the service of all mankind!"—he utters the most path-breaking promise ever made by a black character in comics. And he simultaneously transcends and uplifts his African origins by redeeming himself as a hero fully equal to the Fantastic Four in courage and resourcefulness.

In the end, the most significant landscape in comics is not Africa or any pastoral or rural setting, but rather the city. Comic books, particularly superhero comic books, are about the mythology of urban life. This has been true from Will Eisner's **The Spirit** (whose stereotypical black sidekick, Ebony White, was always problematical as a representative of the African American, but in the tradition of such nonwhite sidekicks as Lothar, who accompanied Mandrake, and Fat Stuff, who was ace pilot Smilin' Jack's foil), which contains some of the best cityscapes ever conceived in a comic book, to Frank Miller's **Batman: The Dark Knight**. (There are exceptions, like the setting of Smallville, a small, Midwestern town in the **Superboy** comics, which should have made it impossible for Clark Kent to hide the fact that he was Superboy from

anyone. The secret identity mechanism in superhero comics only seems possible and plausible in the anonymity of the big city, a noir quality that early superhero and crime comics had and that more recent superhero comics seem to be trying to reinvent.) The Black Panther fights in the African jungle but he ultimately winds up in the city. As a superhero, he is exactly like his white counterparts: he is a vigilante, an exceptional figure who restores order, a redeemer (in this case, with racial overtones). He intervenes because institutions in his society do not work: whether in Africa, where, despite the fact that Africa is depicted as less primitive, it is still a place of few institutions other than royal courts (and this is the Afrocentrist vision of a historicized African culture as well!) of proudly robed, highly muscled people; or whether in America, where democratic institutions do not seem able to protect or serve the people, something that might resonate more with black readers and an aspect of the comic book tradition that black comic books have tried vigorously to exploit. Thus, the comic book superhero, whether white or black, is an extraordinary fantasy figure that combines the far-fetched idealism of heroic, isolated individualism with the cheap cynicism of a world run by corruption, conspiracies, and megalo-maniacs that can only be defeated by extraordinary powers of violence. The fact that these powers are indeed fantastic and cannot exist in the real world undermines any attempt to suggest something useful about the political reality of the world the comic book inhabits.

Even as a black superhero adventure, the superhero comic book

cannot transcend the limitations of the infantile nature of its pulp escapism. The Black Panther became the model for the subsequent black superheroes like Luke Cage, Steel, Black Goliath, and the host of black heroes—from Static, the black adolescent hero who partly resembles early Peter Parker/SpiderMan, and who has a Jewish girlfriend, to Icon, the noble inner-city school teacher—that inhabited Dakota, the mythological urban world of Milestone Comics, probably the most important and famous black-operated comic book company in history.[14] The fact that Milestone Comics, for instance, as with most other black superhero comics, tended to suggest the city as a site of real black social and political problems that the hero helps to alleviate in some way, is not so much an advance for comics but rather a regression to the earliest superhero comic books of the early 1940s, like **The Spirit**, **Superman**, **Captain Marvel**, and **Green Lantern**, where the heroes dealt with real foes of democracy and its institutions, supported liberalism, and stood up for the common people.[15] Or it is a regression to some of the superhero comics of the late 1960s and early 1970s, like the landmark **Green Lantern** #76, April 1970,[16] which returned the city in the superhero comic to something like a real place (at least, something resembling the American city in the popular mind of the late 1960s and early 1970s, troubled, crime-ridden, racially segregated and economically segregated, unable to provide basic services, and violent), not the complete fantasyland of Metropolis and Gotham City that was featured in Superman and Batman comics of the 1950s and 1960s. In either case, it can be argued that the black superhero genre did not reinvent or reimagine the genre of urban superhero comics but simply racialized older aspects of that style of comic book in hopes of attracting a young black audience. It never questioned or challenged the very idea of the superhero as inherently infantile or an inherently ironic authoritarian figure who insisted on flaunting the conventions and institutions of democratic authority. The superhero comic is, in short, always, in the end, a refigured western, a mythology of regeneration through violence and an expression of oddly anti-social civic piety. It is the romance of the sociopath and it is the romance of masculinity.

The presence of black female superheroes like Rocket in the Milestone series is essentially as meaningless as the existence of female superheroes such as Wonder Woman. They are, by and large, not actually women heroes but a sexual fantasy projection (women with impossibly Amazon-like figures, much resembling the fantasies of underground comic innovator Robert Crumb who said he drew most of his women to resemble Sheena the Jungle Queen)[17] built on the frame of male heroic paradigm, the vigilante, the redeemer. (In this sense, male Afrocentrist fantasy urges are little different from male Eurocentrist fantasy urges. Because Black Nationalism and black racial consciousness have seen themselves historically as mostly about the salvation and reclamation of black manhood, Afrocentrist fantasies might be more masculinist than

Eurocentrist fantasies, as they are possibly even more obsessed with the idea of men protecting women because, historically, black men have been denied even the mythology of that act.) We have yet to ask the question seriously in this culture: how do women envision heroism as an imaginative virtue? How would a woman describe a heroic woman? Or, for that matter, what do women see as heroic virtue in a man? Superhero comics, as do comic books generally, remain a masculinist enterprise, which is why they have few women readers.[18]

Three F Productions,
I Spy #2.
Comic book cover
(K.K. Publishers, Inc.)
1967

the influence of television

African Americans' relationship to television changed in the 1960s and this, too, changed the way they were depicted in comics. As the civil rights era progressed and more demands were made by blacks to have popular culture material that reflected their presence in the population and even, to some extent, their taste and interests, and as blacks began to exert more power and influence as a market, prime time television programming began to feature blacks more regularly. Shows like *I Spy* (1965–1968), in which Bill Cosby had a co-star billing, and *The Mod Squad* (1968–1973), where a major black character, played by Clarence Williams III, was an integral part of the show, provided black actors with new roles. *Room 222* (1969–1974), a program about high school, was another important breakthrough with a black character as the lead. *Julia* (1968–1971), which starred Dianne Carroll as a black nurse who is a single mother, was another breakthrough show, the first with a black actress in the lead who was not playing a maid. *The Flip Wilson Show* (1970–1974), the first successful variety show hosted by a black, was yet another breakthrough. *Ironside*, which premiered in 1967, starring Raymond Burr, featured Don Mitchell as a regular cast member. Nichelle Nichols played Lt. Nyota Uhuru—a last name quite in keeping with the times, as it is the Swahili word for freedom—on *Star Trek* (1966–1969). Blacks also had major roles in two of the most important children's programs to air during this time: *Sesame Street* in 1969 with Matt Robinson playing Gordon and Loretta Long as Gordon's wife, Susan, and *The Electric Company* in 1971 with Bill Cosby and Morgan Freeman. But black actors as regulars in a series or with their own shows only reflect part of the change. There were several shows in the 1960s that featured black actors as guest stars and these episodes sometimes dealt with racism, such as the April 26, 1964, episode of the popular western, *Bonanza*, that featured William Marshall as a famous black singer encountering racism, or the episode of *The Name of the Game* that aired on January 24, 1968, featuring Ivan Dixon as a newly elected black mayor facing entrenched racism. Black actor Hari Rhodes, for instance, appeared as a major character in three different episodes of the medical drama, *Ben Casey*, between 1962 and 1965. One of the episodes dealt directly with race.

It has become common for popular television shows to produce comic book versions of themselves. *Maverick*, *Peter Gunn*, *77 Sunset Strip*, *Have Gun*, *Will Travel*, *Perry Mason*, *Zorro*, *The Rifleman*, and many other popular shows of the 1950s and 1960s had comic books based on them, always with photo covers of the stars of the show. Comic book versions of *The Mod Squad* and *I Spy* (both of which ran several issues) not only gave the shows additional publicity with young audiences but also gave the black stars who were featured on the cover of every issue, virtually unheard of in the history of comic books, considerable exposure as well. The black characters were drawn in non-stereotyped ways, usually to resemble the actor, and were

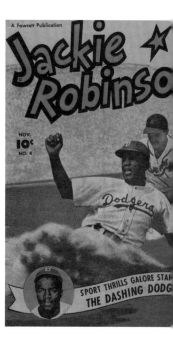

Paramount Pictures Corp.
and Crane
Productions Inc.,
The Young Lawyers.
Comic book cover
(Dell)
January 1970

Harvey Kurtzman, editor,
Frontline Combat #15.
Comic book cover
(EC Comics)
January 1954

Unknown author,
Jackie Robinson vol. I, #4.
Comic book cover
(Fawcett Publishers, Inc.)
November 1950

portrayed, of course, as the character was depicted in the show. Even minor television shows that featured blacks like **The Young Lawyers** (1970–1971), which co-starred Judy Pace, and **Land of the Giants** (1968–1970), which co-starred Don Marshall, had comic books.

Freeing blacks in one pop-culture genre helped to free them in another. But this was not entirely new. Back in the late 1940s and early 1950s, when blacks began to play major league baseball, Fawcett, a major comic book company of the day, produced several comic books starring these black players. Six Jackie Robinson comics were issued between 1949 and 1951, and single-issue comics of Larry Doby, Roy Campanella, Don Newcombe, and Willie Mays were also released during this time. Once again, these books did not draw these men in stereotyped ways, did not have them speak in any sort of debased dialect, and presented them largely in the same way they presented white baseball players in comics, as heroic figures. Comic books tended to respond to and reflect any change that happened to the status of blacks in some other segment of popular culture. At the time these black baseball comics were being produced by an industry player for a mainstream audience, EC Comics, owned by William Gaines

(who was to be driven out of the comic book industry by the reformist zeal to regulate comics in the early 1950s, which led to a comic book code that remained in force in the industry until 1970), produced comics that occasionally featured black characters who were not stereotyped or depicted in a racist manner. Indeed, EC Comics on several occasions dealt forthrightly with the subject of racism. One of the most striking examples of this was the January 1954 issue (#15) of **Frontline Combat**, one of two EC war titles. It featured a black soldier on the cover in combat with whites, virtually unheard of for a war comic, although the Korean War (1950–1953) had effectively ended segregation in the military (following on the heels of Truman's 1948 executive order 9981). EC Comics was the only comics company to write a Korean War story (and a good many Korean War comic book stories were written; combat stories were very popular at the time) that dealt with the issues of integration and racism in the armed services and that featured a black soldier.[19]

Of course, at the heart of all cultural change is a core of ambivalence. Just as blacks were making some headway as actors in the 1960s, shows like **Cowboy in Africa** (1967–1968), **Daktari**

74

(1966–1969), and *Tarzan* (1966–1968) aired, which tended to show Africa as one big game preserve or as a place of nobly primitive people in unfortunate, often inadvertent conflict with the modern or western world, which only wants to help with medicine and education, the two Eurocentrist saviors of the Third World. It has, perhaps, been the most compelling problem for African Americans to try to escape the image of the primitive, an image that has distorted them since the days of nineteenth-century minstrelsy, which presented blacks in popular culture as humorous, simple types, luckily outside the competitive industrialized, labor-driven, money-driven world of whites. It was difficult for blacks to free themselves of the stereotyped ways they were depicted in comics because the stereotyped drawings and speech had been invented and relentlessly reinforced by the world of advertising (blacks became the most famous advertising icons in America between 1880 and 1940) and by the press. This, coupled with a need by the western mind to find some haven, some repose from the "soulless" modern world in a sort of primitivism that seems simple, true, and authentic, has made it difficult for blacks to see themselves clearly as an image, let alone that anyone else should.

robert crumb

The art of Robert Crumb presents a fascinating problem in this regard. Crumb, on the one hand, became the most celebrated artist and writer connected to the underground comics movement of the late 1960s, an attempt to free comics from the commercial domination of DC and Marvel, to free them from the superhero, romance, war, and funny animal motifs that governed their subject matter, to free them from the restrictions and limitations of a child audience. Crumb, without question, revolutionized comics, both the writing and the drawings. But Crumb's depiction of blacks in his work has always been problematical. Crumb tended to portray blacks in highly stereotyped drawings that are reminiscent of the way blacks were depicted in advertising and art at the turn of the century. One might ask, why would an artist who was trying to liberate comic art want to use such retrograde representations of blacks? Yet there has always been an element of the retrograde in Crumb's work. His love of old-fashioned American popular and folk music and his hatred of modern American commercial culture with its strip malls, suburban lawns, and relentless homogenization, are well known. And this nostalgia blends crazily with his fierce self-psychoanalysis and his anarchism to make up the texture of his work. Fredrik Strömberg has suggested that Crumb's most famous black character, Angelfood McSpade, a grotesque, sexualized stereotype of a primitive African woman, is used "to provoke a reaction from the reader, and force them to make up their own minds about their attitudes toward racism."[20] This may be true, but as Crumb's work is so intensely confessional and autobiographical, it would be just as reasonable to say that this character is meant to reflect his own racism, honestly, almost confrontationally, thrown in the face of his audience, just as his sex fantasies, pornographically drawn,

are. It would be simplistic and unhelpful merely to say that Crumb is a racist. He is quite capable of drawing non-stereotyped, non-grotesque blacks, such as he does in his work on the blues, where his discussion of these musicians, their work, and of black people generally does not hint of racism. It would be far fairer to him and his art to suggest that he might be dramatizing his own racism in some way, his own racist fantasies, or collective white fantasies. It must be remembered that in the bohemian world that Crumb operated in in the 1960s, blacks were generally seen exactly as he depicted them in "Angelfood McSpade" or in "Fritz the Cat." They were primitives, highly and freely sexual, unencumbered by the "hang-ups" of civilization, psychopathic, living in the moment. This view of blacks as hip primitives, savage innocents, by the white bohemian world dates back at least as far as the Beats. (One can even find it in the work of blacks, such as some of the novels of Harlem Renaissance writer Claude McKay like **Home to Harlem** [1928] and **Banjo** [1929], both of which predate the Beats.) One has only to read Jack Kerouac's novels like **On the Road**[21] (1957) and **The Subterraneans** (1958) or Norman Mailer's famous essay, "The White Negro" (1957), to know this to be true. Whether Crumb's depiction of blacks is a critique of the Bohemian/Beat/Hippie view or a perverse obsession with it is hard to say. Probably it is a bit of both. After all, Crumb's own preoccupation with old black music shows a predisposition toward seeing black people as interesting and engaging as long as they are not modern or as long as they represent a truly authentic American past.

"Angelfood McSpade" premiered in **Zap Comix** #2 in June 1968.[22] The feature can be read metaphorically: McSpade represents blacks generally (the "Lady of the Races"

SHE'S THE KIND OF CHICK A GUY WOULD BE PROUD TO WALK DOWN THE STREET WITH!

NOT TO MENTION ALL THE THINGS YOU CAN DO TOGETHER AT HOME!!

WHY IS SHE SO HARD TO CATCH UP WITH? WELL, FOR ONE THING, SHE'S ILLEGAL!

GET BACK PUNK!

AND SHE HAS BEEN CONFINED TO THE WILDS OF DARKEST AFRICA. THE OFFICIAL EXCUSE BEING THAT CIVILIZATION WOULD BE THREATENED IF SHE WERE ALLOWED TO DO WHATEVER SHE PLEASED!

CAUTION: UNLAWFUL TO PASS THIS POINT.

BUT THAT HASN'T STOPPED ALOT OF GUYS!

BUT

ANGEL-FOOD!

LET'S GO PUNK!

SIGH

as blacks were called by famed University of Chicago sociologist Robert Ezra Park because of their proclivity to art and oration), simple, innocent, highly sexual, primitive, and exploitable. And she seems indeed, in this script, to be exploited, for all the white men who encounter her want to rape her, although she seems willing enough to be raped in her innocence, probably because she doesn't realize that she is being raped. This interpretation has considerable validity, as the second "Angelfood McSpade," published in the *East Village Other* on October 18, 1968,[23] makes clear. Here she is taken from the jungle by white academic/social scientist types who have come "to assist [her] in becoming a productive member of society."

They ultimately, while she is in the act of licking a toilet upon their instructions, stuff her head in it and sit on her. The character appeared in earlier Crumb features such as "Freak Out Funnies" (*Zap Comix #0*, 1967) and "It's Cosmic" (*Underground Review*, 1967) in much the same way, a highly sexualized, primitive, innocent presence that is abused.

How Crumb presented blacks and race relations in some of his other comics of this period might also be instructive: In "Yin & Yang" (1966), two white male characters encounter a black with a lighted match. They make a pun, saying the black "better quit playing with those matches or he's gonna get 'Watts' coming to him," a reference to the

1965 Watts riot in Los Angeles, one of the worst racial disturbances in American history. The black character gets angry: "Ain't no ofeys [sic] gone ter laugh at dis neegrow!" He then stomps the whites into the ground with each of them saying in turn: "I suppose we deserved this!" "You and your constant racial slurs!" "Oh, well, we're guilty, anyway, right?"[24] "Whiteman" (*Zap Comix* #1, 1967),[25] is a satirical look at the repressed, insecure, and phobia-filled psyche of the white male businessman-type. In the end, he runs into a group of playful African Americans who poke fun at him and tell him, "You jus' a nigger like evva body else!" They tell him he has music in his soul and that he ought to join the parade. The last panel asks, "Will Whiteman join the

parade?" with word balloons surrounding the white man offering reasons why he should and shouldn't join. In "Fritz Bugs Out" (1964–65),[26] a Fritz the Cat episode, the callow Fritz encounters a crow (crows commonly represented blacks in comic art) at a bar. Fritz complains to the crow that he is "hung up, strung out, up tight." He then wishes he were a crow. The crow responds angrily, "You think bein' a crow is a big motherfuggin' Ball! All you cats th' same!" Fritz then talks about his "considerable guilt complex because my kind have brought suffering on your kind." His discussion of his racial guilt leads him back to his original observations about being "hung up, strung out, and up tight." The crow suggests that Fritz "bug out,"[27] that is, abandon himself, throw over his responsibilities. They steal a car, smash it, then wind up at Mildred's Place, where Fritz smokes marijuana and dances with a buxom female crow who sexually intoxicates him. He comes to himself and decides he must tell the masses to revolt, which gets him chased and beaten. This ends the sequence in the story that deals with blacks.

All these comics satirize race relations in the same way: whites are seen as self-conscious hypocrites, who are both obsessed with their racism and their guilt about their racism; blacks are hip innocents (the crow), histrionically angry ("Yin and Yang"), or sexualized primitive morality ("Angelfood McSpade") trapped in stereotypes that they did not make but do not transcend. Is everyone, in the end, really a nigger? Or perhaps maybe everyone ought to be? The problem with this sort of depiction is twofold: First, tying blacks to the primitive, even if as satire, is only to reinforce a view that has dominated thinking about blacks since they came to America, namely, that their appeal is that they are primitive.[28] Second, Crumb's comics suggest that blacks have no view of

themselves apart from how whites see them or fail to see them, which denies them any sense of agency. As such, they never seem to be much more than an ironic foil for white pretensions or the butt end of a cruel racist joke; they become a sort of invisible rapture of the bohemian aesthetic. In short, blacks never cease to be something like holy carnal children. To be sure, despite the limitation of his satire, Crumb is presenting blacks and race relations in more challenging, unnerving ways than most white liberals of the 1960s who wrote comics did. He intensely and richly complicated matters but he did not fundamentally change them.

If the 1960s changed comic books forever, as they changed the status of black people in the United States, it was not without cost. This is not the same as saying that it was not without regret. There is no regret, for there is no longing to go back to something earlier or more authentic. It is perhaps the great irony of the African American presence that others have seen it as signifying an authenticity, a genuineness, a connectedness to something honest and real that does not exist, that never existed, while also seeing it as something wholly false, oppressed, victimized, and distorted that must be corrected, heroicized, or redeemed, a pious search for another type of authenticity that is almost as false and surely as simplistic as the falseness it wishes to defeat. What comic books remind us of is that reality is nothing more than a series, a labyrinth of fabrications, layers of fantasy, willfully sequenced, ordered contrivances and wishes, darkness and light, cheek by jowl, interchangeable. The comic book is the moral text of our social and political disorder, the American kitsch—hymnbook of our anarchist commerce, where we will find, in its pages, what we are, what we think we are, and what we are afraid to see. ✳

1 Maria Reidelbach, *Completely Mad: A History of the Comic Book and Magazine* (Boston: Little, Brown, 1991), 83. The *Hogan's Heroes* parody appeared in *Mad* #108 (January 1967): 4–8, with the savagely bitter "Hochman's Heroes" finale that featured *Hogan's Heroes*–type comedy set at Buchenwald. It appeared before the "Stokely and Tess" parody.

2 Some of the letters that *Mad* published about the parody reveal that several readers did not find the satire funny: one reader was "infuriated. I think that you deliberately insulted the Negro people and mocked the quest for their long-sought-after Freedom following many years of severe persecution and punishment." Another reader complained, "It was grossly unfair to the people and perhaps the whole Civil Rights movement" *Mad* #113 (September 1967), Letters Department, 2. Several letter-writers expressed their enjoyment of the satire and particularly praised its accuracy.

3 Reidelbach, 94.

4 Hollis Alpert, *The Life and Times of Porgy and Bess: The Story of an American Classic* (New York: Knopf, 1990), 263.

5 Henry Louis Gates, Jr., *Thirteen Ways of Looking at a Black Man* (New York: Random House, 1997), 169. Alpert, 260.

6 Alpert, 260–262.

7 Alpert, 121–122. Also, for more on Ellington's reaction to *Porgy and Bess*, see "Ellington on Gershwin's *Porgy and Bess* – and a Response from the Office of Irving Mills," in Mark Tucker, *The Duke Ellington Reader* (New York: Oxford University Press, 1993), 114–118. Ellington denied that he ever made the harsh remarks he is quoted as making in *New Theatre* about *Porgy and Bess*.

8 Although Belafonte refused to play the role of Porgy that he was supposedly offered, he had no problem recording the songs from *Porgy and Bess* with Lena Horne in 1959 for this RCA-Victor album (LOP-1507), clearly meant to exploit the release of the film.

9 Apparently, Jack Kirby invented the Black Panther. See *Tales to Astonish: Jack Kirby, Stan Lee, and the American Comic Book Revolution* (New York: Bloomsbury, 2004), 98–99.

10 Fredrik Strömberg mentions that Lee and Kirby became so concerned about the name, after the rise of the infamously leftist, revolutionary Black Panther Party of Cleaver, Newton, and Seale, that the character was briefly called the Black Leopard in the early 1970s before being reintroduced as the Black Panther in 1973 in the Marvel Comic series, *Jungle Action*. See Fredrik Strömberg, *Black Images in the Comics: A Visual History* (Seattle: Fantagraphics Books, 2003), 129.

11 For more on the tradition of jungle comics, see William W. Savage, Jr., *Comic Books and America, 1945–1954* (Norman: University of Oklahoma Press, 1990), 74–94; Bradford W. Wright, *Comic Book Nation: The Transformation of Youth Culture in America* (Baltimore: The Johns Hopkins Press, 2001), 36–39, 72–75; Bill Black, ed., *The Comic Book Jungle: An Illustrated History of Jungle Comics*, Golden Age Greats, vol. 14 (Longwood, Florida: Paragon Publications, 1999), 2–15, 41–43; *The Golden Age Sheena, Queen of the Jungle* (Longwood, Florida: Paragon Publications, 1999); and Bill Black and Bill Feret, "Sheena Queen of the Jungle: At the Scene of Her Birth – The Whos and Hows," *Good Girl Art Quarterly* (Spring 1001\: 10 ...\:...

12 Just how much the threat of interracial sex or defilement is inherent in the Tarzan/pulp jungle tradition is made apparent in the Tijuana Bible parody of Tarzan. Tijuana Bibles, produced from the 1930s through the 1950s, were eight-page, often poorly drawn pornographic send-ups of famous comic strip and pop-culture figures. The Tarzan Tijuana Bible features an African trying to rape a naked white woman, Dolly, who is rescued by Tarzan, with whom she subsequently has sex. See Bob Adelman, *Tijuana Bibles: Art and Wit in America's Forbidden Funnies, 1930s–1950s* (New York: Simon and Schuster, 1997), 27.

African American artist Larry Fuller's highly pornographic (and for some, highly offensive) *White Whore Funnies* gives the reader a satirical view of interracial sex with highly graphic stories about black men lusting for white women and white women lusting for black men. Fuller was on the margins of the underground comix scene in San Francisco. His first effort was *Ebon*, published in 1970, and mentioned elsewhere in this essay. Fuller also did *Gay Heart Throbs* and *The Adults Only Comix*, both highly pornographic as well. *White Whore Funnies* went through three issues

between 1975 and 1978. In #1, Fuller does two satiric send-ups of jungle comics.

In the first, entitled "Jungle Madness," a white woman, hands bound, is being escorted through the jungle by a group of African men. A Tarzan figure comes to the rescue, defeating the members of the tribe. When the Tarzan figure frees the white woman, far from being grateful, she attacks him, saying, "You Turkey! For 10 weeks I've been trying to get captured and raped by the Fukangas and you have to spoil the whole show." The other called "WhiteGirlManiak Captured!" tells the story of a black convict named Willie Lee Nogoodnik, just released from prison for indecent behavior with white women. He is warned to "stay away from white girls – or else!" He goes to Africa where he feels he will be safe from indulging his obsession because there are no white people. Suddenly, Shestuf, Queen of the Jungle, appears and claims Nogoodnik for her mate. The African tribesmen get jealous: "Us blacks of th' Fierce Mumbweebwees been hittin' on yo' ass for d' las' six years, with no hint of success." So, both Shestuf and Nogoodnik are put in a cannibal's pot to be boiled. The ambiguity of how the racist

are being both made fun of and oddly endorsed in this sort of satire probably made it disturbing to some of its readers.

Robert Kanigher, script,
Werner Roth, art,
Vince Colletta, inks,
Superman's Girlfriend Lois Lane #106.
Comic book cover
(National Periodical Publications, Inc., Carmine Infantino, Publisher under DC)
November 1970

13 Quoted in Shirley Temple Black, *Child Star: An Autobiography* (New York: McGraw-Hill, 1988), 90.

14 For more on Milestone Comics, see Jeffrey A. Brown, *Black Superheroes, Milestone Comics, and their Fans* (Jackson: University Press of Mississippi, 2001). Also see the highly informative special issue of *The Comics Journal* devoted to "Black Comic Artists," *The Comics Journal*, no. 160 (July 1993). In this issue, Nabile Hage, a member of the black collective ANIA, challenged Milestone Comics. "I have nothing against Milestone. I wish them all the best. I just wish they would stop lying by saying they're independent. I don't see how anybody can claim they're independent when they don't own shit. I opened up their book, and it clearly says: 'All characters… the distinct likenesses thereof…' and everything are trademarked DC Comics! That means DC owns everything." (41) A good deal of the significance of Afrocentrist or black nationalist aspiration and pretension is tied to black entrepreneurism and the ability of blacks to exploit and control their own cultural products for their own benefit. Milestone artists accused ANIA of being racist because of their intense black nationalist vision. ANIA artists accused Milestone of being a sell-out and producing insincere black comic art because Milestone was controlled by DC.

15 See Bradford Wright's readings of early superhero comics in *Comic Book Nation*, 7–29.

16 An even more telling comic book, in this regard, is *Superman's Girlfriend Lois Lane* #106 (November 1970). The cover depicts Lois Lane being transformed from white to black. The story chronicles how Lois is given the assignment of writing about Metropolis's Little Africa (which readers of the comic in the early and mid-1960s did not know existed). She finds that she is unable to get any cooperation from the blacks in the neighborhood, who distrust her because she is white. She has Superman take her to his Fortress of Solitude and, through a mechanism, temporarily make her black. She then learns firsthand what black urban life is like and the blacks open up to her. Obviously, the idea of white becoming black to find out what black life is like was borrowed from John Howard Griffin's book, *Black Like Me*, published in 1960. The story is entitled "I Am Curious (Black)," a reference to the controversial, sexually explicit 1967 Swedish film called "I Am Curious (Yellow)," suggesting that the comic is doing something that is taboo breaking just as the film did with its frontal nudity and actual sex. (These particular observations were also made in Strömberg, *Black Images in the Comics*, 151.) Once again, the city is seen as a divided, racially polarized place where the heroics of Superman actually seem out of place and strangely discordant with the texture of the story. Blacks are largely depicted as proud, warm, and good, if slightly misguided in their militancy, despite the travails of living in the ghetto. The question of interracial sex arises here when Lois Lane, who has always, since her creation as a character, wanted to marry Superman, asks him if he would marry her if her blackness remained permanent, making her "an outsider in a white man's world." Superman evades the question by describing his own outsider status as an alien from Krypton, as a person whose "skin is tougher than steel." He then says that he could not marry her because his enemies would use her as a target. But as Lois says to him, "Your skin is the right color." It is of note that Superman does not directly answer the question of whether Lois's race truly matters; he only says that he is "a universal outsider," which is true, but he is also a universal representative of a set of values. What is new here is that the whiteness of Superman is considered not as an expression of something universal but something historically and culturally specific because the story itself has placed him in a culturally specific, historicized world. The story also suggests that Superman, like Lois as a black, is passing for something he isn't. All superhero stories, with their psychological mechanism of the secret identity or alter ego, are, in part, about passing, about seeming to be something that you are not, or the public assumption that some aspect of yourself is your total identity. This sort of concern, simplistically, though sometimes compellingly, rendered in comic stories, would have a particular appeal to children and adolescents, who are, of course, struggling with their own identities. Nonetheless, this Lois Lane story would be seen today by many readers as condescending. It was written by Robert Kanigher

17 For more on Crumb's obsession with Sheena, including a set of panels depicting Sheena taken from *Zap* #10, 1982, see *The Comics Journal Library*, Volume 3: R. Crumb (Seattle: Fantagraphics Books, 2004), 21.

18 There is a growing body of literature dealing with women comic book characters and women comic book artists, most of it by feminist comic book artist and historian, Trina Robbins, a staunch Robert Crumb critic.

19 For more on war comics of the period, see Bradford Wright, *Comic Book Nation*, 109–127, and William Savage, *Comic Books and America, 1945–1954*, 51–65. Wright's account of EC comics can be found on pages 135–152 of *Comic Book Nation*. For more on the unusual nature of EC war comics see the interview with Harvey Kurtzman in *The Comics Journal*, no. 67 (October 1981): 68, 69, 71–73, 75–81, 83–85. The rest of the lengthy interview deals with Kurtzman's career after EC Comics. Kurtzman created and drew most of EC's *Frontline Combat* and *Two-Fisted Tales*.

20 Fredrik Strömberg, *Black Images in the Comics*, 133. "[Crumb's] treatment of blacks is based on the stereotype common to an outdated tradition, but it seems certain that this is a reflection of prejudice than it is a commentary on the prejudice he sees around him." Also see Les Daniels, *Comix: A History of Comic Books in America* (New York: Outerbridge and Dienstfrey, 1971), 171.

21 Crumb read *On the Road* when he was seventeen and was, as would be expected, highly impressed by it. See *The Comics Journal Library*, Volume 3: R. Crumb, (Seattle: Fantagraphics Books, 2004), 19.

22 *The Complete Crumb*, vol. 5 (Seattle: Fantagraphics Books, 1990), 16–19.

23 *The Complete Crumb*, vol. 5, 70.

24 *The Complete Crumb*, vol. 4 (Seattle: Fantagraphics Books, 1989), 20.

25 *The Complete Crumb*, vol. 4, 105–108.

26 *The Complete Crumb*, vol. 3 (Seattle: Fantagraphics Books, 1988), 23–26.

27 "Bugging out" was a popular term during the Korean War, referring to soldiers who abandoned their posts in combat and ran away. It was used particularly to describe the action of black soldiers during the early days of the Korean War who, supposedly, were more likely to run away from battle than whites.

28 A more recent example of Crumb's preoccupation with the black as primitive, particularly the black woman as a highly sexualized (and, thus, aestheticized) being is *HUP* #3 (1989). In "The Story O' My Life," Crumb draws himself dressed as a baby in a carriage wheeled by an Amazon-like German nanny, who ignores him until she discovers that he is a famous artist. They have sex, Crumb fulfilling his fantasies by bending her body in a number of contortionist poses, a typical Crumbian gesture when his work involves sex with women. This urge to depict the humiliation of women through sex also reflects his own guilt that his liberation comes at the expense of his dignity and someone else's. In the final panel, Crumb sees an Amazon-like, highly robust black woman, not stereotypically drawn, who is about to set off to work in the fields. Perhaps she is a slave? She would certainly bring that to mind. In any case, the infantile Crumb (dressed a baby), thinks "Dear Jeeziz God in heaven what a primal lookin' thing! Oh man! Look at those brown shiny legs! The–The sensuous swing of her hips!…"

A Chronology of

comics &
the graphic arts

compiled and edited by

D.B. *Dowd* and *Melanie Reinert*

with contributions from *Gerald Early*, *Todd Hignite*,
and *Daniel Raeburn*

Significant
artists and works

Advances
in printing
technology

Developments
in distribution

Visual
innovations

Beyond the frame

Development
of underground
comics

Development
of animation

African
Americans
in comics

1380　The Bois Protat, the earl
known woodcut block i
the West, is drawn and c

circa
1440–1450

Johannes Gutenberg develops a reliab
method of printing from moveable typ

circa
1480

Martin Schongauer produces the entertainingly ghastly engraving *The Temptation of St. Anthony*, arguably the first work of horror illustration ever printed.

Attributed to Albrecht Dürer, "On Predestination of God," from ***Das Narrenschiff (The Ship of Fools)*** by Sebastian Brant. Woodcut, 1494.

1460–1500

Secular illustrated books begin to appear. Important examples printed from woodcut blocks and moveable type include Pfister's *Book of Fables*, 1461.

circa
1420–1430

The medium of decorative engraving on curved surfaces practiced by silversmiths and armorers (called *niello*) makes a transition to flat pieces of metal for purposes of reproduction. Copper engraving and intaglio printing are born.

1497–1498

Albrecht Dürer (1471–1528) publishes the *Apocalypse*, a sustained pictorial translation of the Book of Revelation, rendered in woodcut.

1493

Anton Koberger publishes the *Nuremberg Chronicle*.

1473

Gunther Zanier of Augsburg instructs guild cutters to work from blocks that are type-measure wide. The type and woodcut illustrations for his edition of *Speculum Humanae Salvationis* (*Mirror of Man's Salvation*) are printed simultaneously, adding speed and flexibility to the process.

1513

Urs Graf produces the first etching plate, by coating copper with wax, scratching through it, and dunking the metal in acid.

The resulting chemically produced grooves are filled with thick black ink. The plate is printed intaglio by smashing soft wet paper into the grooves, which read as lines on the print. Dürer adopts the medium.

1494

Sebastian Brant's *Das Narrenschiff* (*The Ship of Fools*) is published. The book is composed of moralistic poems accompanied by comical woodcut illustrations.

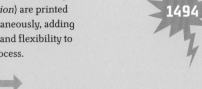
circa
1450

Printer-publishers develop the broadsheet, an early print vehicle that combines printed text and woodcut illustration on a single page.

Broadsheets are sold at pilgrimage sites, fairs, and in urban locations across Europe. These early ancestors of the tabloids convey saints' biographies, moralizing ballads, and sensationalist news stories. Broadsheets are well suited to propagandistic purposes, and are thus employed especially during the German Reformation in the early 16th century.

1460–1500

Printed, woodcut-illustrated books, didactic but not strictly from religious sources, find a popular audience in the educated upper and merchant classes of Western Europe.

pre-1800

1600 Etching is refined and popularized in the early 17th century by Callot and Rembrandt, among others.

1735 William Hogarth (1697–1764) publishes *A Rake's Progress*, a moralizing suite of engravings with captions. This and other Hogarth works, e.g., *A Harlot's Progress* (1732) and *Marriage A-la-Mode* (1745), are widely pirated.

circa 1730 Caricaturists in France and England place conversational text inside loosely drawn, breath-like shapes.

These predecessors of the comic "word balloon" bring the content of an external caption into the visual composition.

1730–1750

Hogarth creates captioned suites of engravings that uphold sustained narratives through series of melodramatic illustrated vignettes.

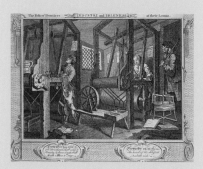

William Hogarth, "The Fellow 'Prentices at their Looms," from *Industry and Idleness*, plate 1. Engraving, 1747.

circa 1750–1850

The stylization of the human face and figure in the work of French and English caricaturists such as James Gillray, George Cruikshank, and Thomas Rowlandson can be seen as a forerunner to "cartoon" exaggeration.

1735 Hogarth successfully lobbies Parliament to pass the Engravers' Copyright Act of 1735, an early intellectual property protection for artists.

pre-1800

circa

1770

Thomas Bewick, a copper engraver, discovers that fine, durable relief printing surfaces can be produced by using metal engraving tools on hard end-grain wood blocks.

"White line engraving" brings high-speed printing to book and periodical illustration. Between 1830 and 1850 wood engraving matures into the first truly industrial image production system.

1796–1799

Francisco de Goya (1746-1828) publishes *Los Caprichos*, a satirical suite of captioned etchings. *Los Caprichos* represents one of the first uses of aquatint on an artistically significant project.

1794

William Blake (1757-1827) self-publishes *Songs of Innocence and of Experience*, an idiosyncratic book of poetry.

Thomas Bewick,
"The Ibex,"
from *A General History of Quadrupeds*.
Wood engraving, c. 1790.

1790

Thomas Bewick publishes *A General History of Quadrupeds*. This book and the subsequent *History of British Birds* (1797) mark the first significant uses of wood engraving in book illustration.

1760-1780

The aquatint, a technique for achieving tones on an etching plate, is invented.

A primitive tonal screen is produced by melting specks of rosin on a heated copper plate. The rosin hardens into an acid resist. Value is controlled by the length of time in the acid bath; the longer the "bite," the darker the tone. Before long, multiple-plate aquatints are used with standard colors (the primaries plus black) to print the first "process," or optical, color (e.g., blue printed over yellow yields green).

1798

Alois Senefelder accidentally discovers the principles of lithography by writing out a list for his laundry woman on a piece of stone.

1780–1810

James Gillray, a failed painter, forsakes his British Academy training and begins to produce satirical etchings. His efforts—viciously funny, inventive, and visually sophisticated—help to found the field of modern political cartooning.

Benjamin West,
"Angel of the Resurrection,"
from **Specimens of Polyautography**,
published by Philipp André.
Lithograph, 1801.

1801–1807

Philipp André commissions and
publishes *Specimens of Polyautography*,
the first major artistic use of lithography.
Contributors include Benjamin West
and Thomas Stothard.

1800–1830

British illustrator and caricaturist
George Cruikshank's (1792–1878)
political caricatures find widespread
popularity. He often uses balloon devices
to portray speech.

1800S

Thomas Rowlandson,
The Loves of the Fox and the Badger
or The Coalition Wedding.
Hand-colored etching, 1784.

1812

Thomas Rowlandson (1756–1827), a British Academy–trained artist, printmaker, and caricaturist, publishes *The Tour of Doctor Syntax in Search of the Picturesque*, a satirical narrative suite of etchings illustrating William Combe's poem.

1810–1830

The inspired savageries of British caricature as practiced during the Georgian era gradually give way to more genteel cartooning in family-oriented magazines. British caricaturists start to explore comic stories in serial formats. By 1830, Paris begins to emerge as a leading hotbed of political caricature.

1810s

1820-1840

Improved, affordable print technology, rising literacy rates, and the growth of "leisure incomes" for the middle and working classes augment the production of publications in Europe and America.

1829 Charles Philipon founds a caricature shop, La Maison Aubert, in Paris.

Thomas Rowlandson,
"Death of Punch,"
from *The Third Tour of Dr. Syntax: In Search of a Wife*, by William Combe.
Hand-colored etching and aquatint, 1821.

1827 John James Audubon publishes large folios of *Birds of America*. The work is one of the last significant publications printed intaglio. Later editions are produced with lithography.

Rodolphe Töpffer,
Monsieur Pencil.
Autolithography
(lithographic process), 1840.

1820S

circa
1830–1870

The birth of lithographic picture publishing. Print shops in Europe and America produce and market lithographs of various paper grades across a spectrum of subjects. Such a wide range of images and fine gradations in quality and pricing appeal to buyers of different social standing, from the working class to the wealthy.

1839

Louis Jacques Mandé Daguerre (working in part from progress made by the late Joseph Niépce) patents the daguerreotype.

The photographic revolution commences. Two key influences: photography leads directly to the development of new commercial image-printing techniques; and photographic vision leads to new ways of designing and framing images, visible from Degas to the adventure comics of the 1930s.

1832

Philipon launches *le Charivari*, another lithographic caricature journal, with a less outspoken, less political focus.

1830–1840

Honoré Daumier (1808–1879), painter, periodical illustrator, and popular caricaturist, begins creating drawings for Charles Philipon, publisher of the caricature journals *la Caricature* and *le Charivari*.

Daumier contributes many satirical series of prints, which are printed in journals and sold separately to collectors.

1830

Philipon begins publishing his political journal *la Caricature*, illustrated with lithographs. He is repeatedly censored and fined by the French government.

1834

Currier and Ives is founded by Nathaniel Currier and James Ives.

The company produces thousands of cheap lithographic prints on a wide array of topics throughout the 19th century.

circa
1840–1850

European publishers steal Töpffer's idea, bootlegging his comic stories and illustrations across Europe. Publishers in America pirate the bootlegs.

rca
830–1840

odolphe Töpffer publishes s early picture stories including *istoire de M. Jabot* (1835), *s Amours de M. Vieux Bois* *837*), *Histoire de M. Crépin* (1837), d *Monsieur Pencil* (1840). These umorous books appeal to both ults and children.

1830–1840

Töpffer represents the passage of time and the motion of his characters by breaking his illustrated narrative sequences into series of crudely drawn panels.

Visual gags and action sequences are broken down, motion by motion, into multiple frames, foreshadowing both comics and animation. He maximizes the impact of his repetitive humor and "shaggy-dog" stories by juxtaposing in adjacent frames simultaneous scenes set in different locales.

1830S

1841 William Henry Fox Talbot publicly introduces the calotype, which produces repeated positive images from a single negative.

1843 A British periodical breathes new life into the word "cartoon" by mocking official art. In response to an exhibition of preparatory sketches for large murals (the traditional usage of the term) to be installed in Parliament, *Punch* publishes a round of answering "cartoons," each of which includes an image plus a witty caption.

1842 *The London Illustrated News* is founded.

1841 The comic magazine *Punch* begins publication in London, aiming its humor at a literary, educated class.

1840-1850

Cham (Amédée de Noé, 1818–1879) launches an extremely productive career as a caricaturist and illustrator for the comic journals of Paris, including Philipon's publications.

For his journal submissions, caricaturist Cham sometimes works in a *macédoine* format, which resembles a comic strip in its layout of twelve drawings to a page.

1840S

1852

William Henry Fox Talbot patents an early version of the photogravure process, which allows for the reproduction of grayscale images.

The yes/no graphic language of black and white, manually manipulated to achieve optical grays via hatching, heretofore basic to relief printing, is challenged.

Winslow Homer,
"The Inaugural Procession at Washington Passing the Gate of the Capitol Grounds,"
illustration from *Harper's Weekly*.
Wood engraving, 1861.

1855   *Frank Leslie's Illustrated Newspaper* is founded.

1857   *Harper's Weekly*, an illustrated newspaper in direct competition with *Leslie's*, is founded.

circa **1865**
Wilhelm Busch (1832–1908) produces *bilderbogen*, or captioned picture stories that tell darkly humorous moral tales about the fates of naughty children.

circa **1860**
Thomas Bolton produces a wood engraving from an image on a photo-sensitized wood block in an early experiment with photographic reproduction in illustration.

Currier and Ives,
***Rounding a Bend on the Mississippi,
The Final Salute***.
Chromolithograph, c. 1866.

circa
1860–1870

Drawing on Töpffer, Gustave Doré, and the legacy of European caricature, cartoonists and illustrators including Busch and Duval begin to develop, establish, and codify various visual conventions that communicate motion in a static image.

1867
Marie Duval and husband Charles Henry Ross develop and illustrate *Ally Sloper*, one of the first repeated and serialized comic characters in Europe, for *Judy* magazine. *Sloper*'s format jumps between compartmentalized semi-narrative vignettes and large cartoons.

1865
Busch produces *Max und Moritz*. It is widely translated and pirated.

1865
Sir John Tenniel (1820–1914), staff illustrator for the humor magazine *Punch*, is recruited by author Lewis Carroll to illustrate the children's book *Alice's Adventures in Wonderland* and its 1871 sequel *Through the Looking Glass*.

1860S

Eadweard Muybridge,
The Gallop.
Series of photographs, c. 1877.

The New Watercolor Society
is formed by a group
of illustrators in Britain,
including John Tenniel,
Randolphe Caldecott, and
Kate Greenaway. They
imagine, wrongly, that the
organization and its
exhibitions will grant them
legitimacy in the eyes of
the Royal Academy.

Thomas Nast,
"The Third Term Panic,"
editorial illustration from ***Harper's Weekly***.
Wood engraving, November 7, 1874.

Wilhelm Busch,
images from ***Die Fromme Helene***.
Woodcut, 1872.

1877

Charles Reynaud invents
the praxinoscope, building
on William George Horner's
zoetrope of 1834.

The device, one in a developing
tradition of rotating motion projection
machines, shows a brief series of
images in quick succession, creating
the illusion of animation.

circa
1870–1930

"Chalk talk" begins.

Illustrators and cartoonists from Thomas Nast
to Winsor McCay appear on the lecture and
vaudeville circuits. Chalk talks combine rapid
drawing at a board with witty narration;
the fare includes signature characters as well
as visual stories and puns. Popular illustrators
and cartoonists are transformed into celebrity
showmen.

1877

Eadweard Muybridge
(1830–1904) photographs
a horse in motion.

Stop-motion photography influences
printed cartoons and proto-comics
as well as painting and illustration.
In 1879 Muybridge invents the
zoöpraxiscope, a variation on the
zoetrope, to project brief motion
sequences of his celebrated beasts.

1874

Thomas Nast (1840–1902)
draws the "Republican
elephant" symbol for the
first time.

As with many of his other visual icons,
such as Uncle Sam, the Tammany
tiger, and his interpretation of Santa
Claus, it is absorbed into the language
of cartooning. Nast's editorial
illustrations change public opinion
and goad politicians into action.

R.F. Outcault,
Letter to Library of Congress
seeking copyright for Yellow Kid character.
Ink, pencil, watercolor,
and blue pencil on paper, 1896.

1884 The McClure syndicate is founded.

1884 Albert Blake Dick invents mimeography.

In 1886 Thomas A. Edison (1847–1931) develops the first mimeograph machine in partnership with Dick.

1883 Joseph Pulitzer purchases the *New York World* and begins recruiting a powerhouse staff of writers and artists.

1883 Irving Bachellor creates the first syndicate company.

1880–1890

Halftone printing processes begin to make commercial appearances.

While experiments with various dot and line systems had begun as early as 1850, the problem requires decades to solve. Cross-line halftone illustrations appear in newspapers beginning in 1880. Georg Meisenbach patents a line screen in 1882. Frederick Ives patents a dot screen in 1886, which Max Levy successfully refines in the 1890s. The process transforms the illustrated publishing industry.

1880S

circa
1890-1895

Entertainment-focused
Sunday color
supplements appear.

They provide a showcase for
the talents of staff illustrators
and cartoonists.

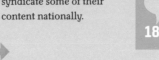
1895 The major New York
newspapers begin to
syndicate some of their
content nationally.

1899 Sigmund Freud
publishes his theory
*The Interpretation of
Dreams*, a topic that
inspires popular
newspaper comics.

1895 William Randolph Hearst
purchases the *New York
Journal* and begins an
aggressive competition with
Pulitzer's paper that gives
rise to the term "yellow
journalism."

1890 The commercial four-color
"process color" printing
process debuts across
Europe and America.

From 1892, printed color cartoons are
available in newspapers in Chicago
and New York. The advent of process
color, combined with the innovations
of photo-engraving and photo-
lithography begin to eliminate the
artisan from the coloring process.

1896 Outcault takes his Yellow Kid
to Hearst's *New York Journal*.

A legally disputed version of the
character continues on at the
New York World after his departure.
The ghosted feature is drawn by
George Luks.

1896 Outcault attempts to
copyright his character
the Yellow Kid, but the
protection he receives is
minimal.

He subsequently creates a truly
profitable licensed character,
Buster Brown, in 1902.

1895–1896

R.F. Outcault develops his
character, the "Yellow Kid,"
in the pages of the
New York World.

1895–1897
The Yellow Kid's text-
covered shirt serves as his
method of communication.

1891 Edison develops the
kinetiscope, an early
automated film projector.

1896 Lithographic stones
are replaced by
simulated limestone.

Zinc and aluminum plates
are developed for use in the new
rotary presses.

1890s

1902

Outcault begins *Buster Brown* in the *New York Herald*.

Characters from the defunct *Yellow Kid* make appearances in the strip.

1906

American Ira Rubel invents the first offset lithographic press.

Early lithographic presses printed directly from stone or plate to paper. An offset press moves the ink from plate to paper in two steps, using a drum or cylinder to do so. Direct transfer prints must be drawn reverse-reading, or backwards; offset plates are drawn "right-reading."

Winsor McCay, *Little Nemo in Slumberland*, from the *New York Herald*. Comic strip detail, 1905.

1905

The cinematic framing and pacing of his visual narratives reflect Winsor McCay's avid interest in early animation technology.

1900–1910

Newspaper comic strips implement word balloons and frame-by-frame formats that break the narrative into individual chronological scenes, much like a film storyboard.

1900-1945

The "Golden Age of Newspaper Comics," as commonly defined.

1900

Six major syndicate companies control most newspaper comics distribution. Of these, Hearst, McClure, and World Color Co. alone control approximately 75% of the industry.

1905

Winsor McCay (1871-1934) begins the newspaper comic strip *Little Nemo in Slumberland*. Nemo's surreal adventures raise comic illustration to a new level.

1904

Outcault licenses the name Buster Brown to the Brown Shoe Company of St. Louis.

The Buster Brown logo premieres at the 1904 World's Fair in St. Louis.

1908-1913

The Ashcan School emerges in New York. Led by Robert Henri and including painters John Sloan, William Glackens, and George Luks, the group explores urban life in muscularly realist, thickly applied oils.

1900S

1903

Winsor McCay's cartoon, *Tales of the Jungle Imps*, concerning the misadventures of a group of stereotyped African "savage" characters, runs in the *Cincinnati Enquirer*.

1907

Bud Fisher's (1885-1954) *A. Mutt*, later *Mutt and Jeff*, begins running in the *San Francisco Chronicle*.

As the strip is syndicated and grows in popularity, Fisher becomes one of the first cartoonists to subcontract his production labor to other artists.

John Sloan,
cover illustration for **The Masses**.
Lithograph, June 1914.

1913

Bringing Up Father by
George McManus
(1884–1954) starts its run in
Hearst-owned newspapers.

1918

Gasoline Alley by Frank
King (1883–1969) begins
running in the *Chicago
Tribune*.

Baby Skeezix and the characters
surrounding him age in real time as the
years go on, lending a new dimension
to the comics experience.

1911

Winsor McCay leaves the
New York Herald after a
lucrative offer from Hearst
draws him to the *New York
American*.

circa
1910-1920

The first sustained efforts
at cinematic animation
appear in theaters and
vaudeville acts.

Many of the characters in these early shorts come
directly from the newspaper comics pages. By the
1920s American animation has taken off as a new
entertainment industry, growing up alongside and
intertwined with the new comics market.

1911

Scribner's Classics
publishes an edition of
Robert Louis Stevenson's
Treasure Island with
illustrations by N.C. Wyeth.

1914

Earl Hurd patents the
transparent animation cel,
which enables animators to
separate the production of
static background art from
the drawing of character
movement.

Cels are stacked and photographed
together, producing a unified image.

1919

Felix the Cat, created by Otto
Messmer (1892–1983) and the
developed product of Pat Sullivan
Studios, debuts in the silent
animated short *Feline Follies*.

References to blackface humor, minstrelsy,
and stereotyped black characters are
a frequent source of visual punchlines in many
early cartoons, including the Felix series.

1911

The Masses, a radical
leftist periodical,
is founded. The magazine
employs politically
progressive artists (e.g.,
John Sloan, Reginald
Marsh, Rockwell Kent,
and Stuart Davis) to
produce cover illustrations
and cartoons.

1910S

1929 Dell Publishing issues *The Funnies*, a magazine filled with original comic strip material in a tabloid format.

circa **1927** Walt Disney creates an early form of storyboarding – the systematic planning of screen images in relation to a script – and applies it in the development of early Mickey Mouse shorts *Steamboat Willie* and *Plane Crazy*.

1923 Felix gets his own comic strip, moving in reverse of the increasingly liquid flow of titles and characters from comic strips to animation.

circa **1929** Advertisers begin reprinting newspaper comic strips in cheaply produced book formats for promotional tie-ins to their products.

1928 Walt Disney releases *Steamboat Willie*, the first animated short with a synchronized soundtrack, and Mickey Mouse's second theatrical release.

1920–1940

American advertisers begin to use the comics format and licensed characters to market their products.

1929 Hergé (Georges Remi, 1907–1983) publishes *The Adventures of Tintin in The Land of the Soviets*, an early adventure comic, in a Belgian newspaper.

circa **1928** RCA transmits the first experimental television broadcast: an image of Felix the Cat.

1920s

Frank King,
Gasoline Alley,
from the *Chicago Tribune*.
Comic strip panels, 1931.

 **1934** *Terry and the Pirates*, a newspaper strip by Milton Caniff (1907–1988), embodies the adventure comics genre.

 1938 Chester Carlson invents electrostatic reproduction, otherwise known as the Xerox process.

The first copy machine appears in 1949, and the first automatic copier follows in 1959. The 1960s see the rise of the increasingly affordable copy machine as an office fixture.

 1934 *Flash Gordon*, an adventure comic with a pulp science-fiction theme is created by Alex Raymond (1909–1956) and drawn by several illustrators during its course, including Austin Briggs (1908–1973).

 1939 Atlas/Timely comics, which later becomes Marvel Comics, is founded.

 1937 Harry Donenfeld and Major Malcolm Wheeler-Nicholson launch *Detective Comics*.

 1933 Eastern Color Printing publishes *Funnies on Parade*, an advertising premium for Procter & Gamble, and the first publication with the scale and proportions of today's comic book.

 **1931** *Dick Tracy* by Chester Gould (1900–1985) begins running in newspapers in Chicago and New York.

The strip influences subsequent superhero strips with its pantheon of villains, and reflects the growing genre of detective and crime comics.

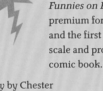 **1930–1950** Pornographic comic books nicknamed "Tijuana Bibles" are popular.

 1933 Dell Publishing Company is founded.

 **1938** Joe Siegel and Jerry Shuster's Superman appears in *Action Comics* and launches a wave of copycat superhero comics.

1939 Bob Kane's *Batman* appears in *Detective Comics*.

1932 Whitman Publishing prints *The Adventures of Dick Tracy*, the first Big Little Book.

 1937 *Prince Valiant* by Hal Foster (1892–1982) begins running in Sunday newspapers.

1930 A *Gasoline Alley* strip places Skeezix and Uncle Walt inside a series of environments mimicking Cubist, Post Impressionist, and Surrealist artworks, and other "modern" art movements.

1936 Photo-Lettering Inc. becomes one of the first companies to regularly use photo-mechanical processes in type-setting.

1930S

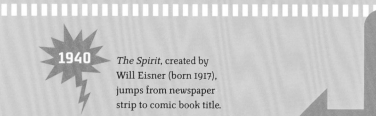

1947

African American journalist Orrin Evans publishes *All-Negro Comics* #1, the only issue and the first attempt by blacks to publish a comic book series.

1940

The Spirit, created by Will Eisner (born 1917), jumps from newspaper strip to comic book title.

1941

Jack Cole's (1914-1958) violently slapstick superhero comic *Plastic Man* appears in *Police Comics*.

1947

The explicitly violent *True Crime Comics*, edited by Jack Cole, debuts with its controversial story "Murder, Morphine, and Me."

The series and issue are later cited by Fredric Wertham in *Seduction of the Innocent* as examples of the bloody violence to which he objects. Cole goes on to provide cheesecake illustrations to Hugh Hefner's *Playboy* magazine.

1940

Dell Publishing begins printing Disney comics in an exclusive licensing deal with Walt Disney Productions.

1942

Maxwell Gaines, once of Eastern Color Printing, founds Educational Comics, or EC.

1940

Lev Gleason Comics, publisher of *Crime Does Not Pay,* is founded.

1940-1945

Many comics publish patriotic stories during World War II. Heroes such as Captain America appear to boost morale on the home front and in the Armed Forces.

1947

Maxwell Gaines is killed. William Gaines, the surviving son, assumes control of EC, which he renames "Entertaining Comics."

EC banks its future on the new genres of horror and crime comics by introducing a formula for packaging titillating narratives. The company's comics become a specific target of Wertham's quest to clean up the industry's content.

1940S

1949

Fawcett begins publishing a series of Jackie Robinson comics. This leads to other black baseball players being featured in special comics that are devoted to their exploits.

1946

Broadcast television begins in America.

1950–1960

Animated programs appear on television, often with heavy advertising tie-ins to children's products such as toys and breakfast cereals.

UPA's *Gerald McBoing Boing* airs on television from 1956–1958. It is followed by Jay Ward's *Rocky and His Friends* (1959) and Hanna-Barbera's primetime animated series, *The Flintstones* (1960). These cartoons use a limited animation style with highly simplified characters and minimalized motion.

1950

The quietly funny newspaper strip *Peanuts* is created by Charles Schulz (1922–2000).

1952

The first issue of Harvey Kurtzman's *Mad* is published.

1953-1954

Congressional hearings investigate the effects of comics on juvenile delinquency. William Gaines and Fredric Wertham testify. The committee rules that the industry must self-regulate content.

circa
1950–1960

The troubled comics industry sheds companies and titles as the censorship of the Comics Code Authority affects production and sales.

circa
1950–1960

Television's popularity opens the door for TV animation and live-action adaptations of comic characters' adventures.

1955

The Comics Code Authority stamp appears on approved comics titles in a strict form of self-imposed censorship.

The new code curtails the success and popularity of many companies as their content is diluted or banned entirely.

1954

Psychiatrist Fredric Wertham details the alleged effects on children of gratuitous violence and graphic sexuality in comics in his book *Seduction of the Innocent*.

1950

Fawcett publishes three issues of *Negro Romance*.

1954

EC Comics' *Frontline Combat* shows an integrated U.S. combat company on its cover.

1950S

1961

Marvel Comics' Stan Lee (born 1922) and returning artist Jack Kirby (1917–1994) create the Fantastic Four and begin a new generation of superheroes.

1967–1968

Robert Crumb uses stereotypical representations of African Americans in comix such as "Angelfood McSpade."

1967

Mad publishes a "Special Racial Issue" that includes the parody "Stokely and Tess," a satirical send-up of the civil rights movement.

1962

Stan Lee and Steve Ditko create Spider-Man for Marvel Comics.

1961

Jack Chick begins producing his religious tracts as small comic books, beginning with *A Demon's Nightmare.*

1966

Stan Lee and Jack Kirby introduce the African superhero the Black Panther in *Fantastic Four* #52 and #53.

1968

College student Garry Trudeau creates the prototype for his newspaper strip *Doonesbury*, called *Bull Tales*, which runs in the *Yale Daily News*. Two years later, *Doonesbury* debuts in twelve newspapers in the United States, a number that grows to 1,400 over the next three decades. Trudeau's groundbreaking strip often runs on editorial pages instead of in the "funnies."

Trudeau wins the 1975 Pulitzer Prize for his editorial cartoons.

1969–1972

Graduate students and faculty at UCLA develop an experimental computer network called ARPANET, a direct ancestor of the Internet.

1960–1970

Roy Lichtenstein and others in the American Pop Art movement appropriate comic imagery.

1967

Robert Crumb begins publishing *Zap Comix.*

1960S

Jay Ward and Bill Scott, "Rocket Fuel Formula," ***Rocky and Bullwinkle and Friends***, episode 1. Animation still, 1959.

1970

Paul Orfalea opens the first Kinko's near the University of California at Santa Barbara—with a single copy machine.

1972

Ralph Bakshi directs *Fritz the Cat*, the first x-rated, full-length animated feature film. Though based on characters and events originating from his comic strip of the same name, Robert Crumb disowns the movie adaptation.

1976

Fantagraphics Books is founded by Gary Groth and Kim Thompson. The company will grow to become one of the most important publishers of underground comix, art and alternative comics, and quality reprints of vintage comics titles.

1970

Philip Guston's show at the Marlborough Gallery in New York unveils his comic-influenced style of painting.

1978

Superman the Movie, starring Christopher Reeve as the "Man of Steel," appears in theaters.

1960s

The underground comix movement spreads, powered by a generation of cartoonists critical of the censorship and "assembly-line" aesthetic that characterized the Comics Code Authority era.

1976

The first *American Splendor* comic by Harvey Pekar is published and becomes an underground hit.

Stan Lee, scenarist, and Jack Kirby, illustrator, *Fantastic Four* #99 (Marvel Comics). Comic book cover, 1970.

1970s

1982

Love and Rockets, the work of brothers Gilbert, Jaime, and Mario Hernandez, is published. It is one of the most important titles of the "alternative" period.

1989

Batman, a film directed by Tim Burton, is released by Warner Studios.

Jaime Hernandez,
"We want the World and we want it Bald," from
Love and Rockets #45
(Fantagraphics Books).
Comic book panel, 1994.

1980

Art Spiegelman and Françoise Mouly edit and publish *Raw*, an avant-garde comic book anthology. *Raw* includes serialized installments of *Maus*, a biographical chronicle of Spiegelman's parents' experiences during the Holocaust.

1981

IBM releases its first personal computer, the PCI.

circa 1988

The mini-comics movement grows out of the popularity of DIY.

Individual cartoonists write, illustrate, reproduce, bind, and distribute small runs of their own titles using readily available copying technology.

1987

Adobe Illustrator, an advanced vector graphic design program, is released. It allows for the creation of simple, mathematically derived graphic forms on the computer, for desktop publishing and printing.

1984

Apple releases the Macintosh, the first affordable personal computer with a Graphical User Interface.

1987

Quark XPress, a high-end layout software program, is released.

1980S

1993 Scott McCloud's book *Understanding Comics: The Invisible Art* is published, followed by *Reinventing Comics* in 2000.

1990-2000

Classic-comic reprint projects flourish alongside new work by the most talented generation of cartoonists North America has seen since the 1930s.

Artists like Art Spiegelman, Matt Groening, Charles Burns, Daniel Clowes, Seth, Gary Panter, Chris Ware, and Gary Baseman attract significant attention. Gallery exhibitions attempt to legitimize the craft of cartooning, often with the disastrous premise of how "influential" they are on "real art."

circa
1996–1999

Congressional deregulation lowers the cost of technologies such as fiber optics, high-speed lines, cable modems, and DSL.

1992 Milestone Comics, an all-black division of DC Comics, is formed.

1996 Bill Watterson ceases publication of his newspaper strip *Calvin and Hobbes*, which had run nationally since 1985.

1990 The film *Dick Tracy* is released, directed by and starring Warren Beatty in the title role.

1997 Milestone Comics ceases regular publication.

1993 Fantagraphics Books begins publishing Chris Ware's *Acme Novelty Library* series.

1998 The website usscatastrophe.com, an online distributor of mini-comics, is founded.

1986–1992

Art Spiegelman publishes his graphic novel *Maus* in two volumes, winning a special Pulitzer Prize in 1992.

1995 Microsoft releases Comic-sans, a digital font created by Vincent Connare.

1994–1998

The Internet reaches the mainstream. Web comics and web animation begin to flourish.

1990 Adobe Photoshop, a bitmap-based graphic editing program, is released.

1999 Chris Ware is nominated for an Eisner award in the category of "Best Lettering," but loses.

1990-2000

The introduction of design software for the PC coupled with the distribution possibilities of the Internet result in some cartoonists gearing their work toward an online audience. Web comics are born.

1995 The Federal Networking Council creates an official definition for the term "Internet."

1993 Several independent black comic book creators form ANIA (Swahili for "protect and defend").

1996 Jonathan Gay develops FutureSplash Animator, which becomes Flash 1.0 when distributed by Macromedia.

1990s

Chris Ware,
Jimmy Corrigan,
The Smartest Kid on Earth
(Fantagraphics Books)
Comic book panel, 2000.

2005–2006

The European tradition of political caricature collides with Islamic fundamentalism in the shocking "Cartoon Riots" of 2006.

The culture editor for *Jyllands-Posten*, a Danish newspaper, commissions and prints a series of political cartoons on the religious figure of Mohammed, central to Islam. The effort is designed to tweak fundamentalist sensibilities, but Islamic proscriptions against representations of the Prophet prove to be more powerful than bargained for. A local controversy ensues. Ambassadors from Islamic countries appeal to the Danish government, unsuccessfully, for legal action against the newspaper. A delegation of Danish imams tours the Middle East to market the blasphemy to other Muslim audiences. Subsequent reprintings of the cartoons spark riots across the Islamic world. More than 130 people are killed in clashes, primarily in Nigeria, Libya, Pakistan, and Afghanistan. The Danish cartoonists are driven into hiding.

2004

Mainstream bookstores are increasingly devoted to the graphic novel, setting aside significant floor space for American serial compilations and long form compositions. This development is partly fueled by Western demand for Japanese comics, or *manga*.

2000–2001

The dot-com bubble bursts, forcing many online business ventures to close down or rethink their strategies.

Start-up animation and comics-based businesses are adversely affected; most content providers go belly up.

2002–2005

Small-scale animation and comics projects return to the Internet, in mostly non-commercial forms.

2007

The National Cartoon Museum (formerly the International Museum of Cartoon Art) is slated to open its doors in New York's Empire State Building.

2005

The "Masters of American Comics" show opens at the Hammer Museum and the Museum of Contemporary Art, Los Angeles. A massive exhibition devoted to twentieth-century newspaper strips and comic books, the show marks a first attempt to establish an art historical canon for comic artists.

2001

Daniel Clowes adapts his graphic novel *Ghost World* into a screenplay for the motion picture of the same title, directed by Terry Zwigoff.

2003–2006

Comic book superheroes fly off the pages of their books and onto the silver screen with increasing frequency.

Serial film franchises are built around Marvel's X-Men and Spider-Man; *The Fantastic Four* debuts in 2005. Dark Horse's *Hellboy* storms theaters in 2004. The DC Batman franchise spawns the regrettable spin-off *Catwoman* (2004) and the more successful *Batman Begins* (2005). After a long absence from theaters, the Man of Steel reappears in *Superman Returns* (2006). The comics movies from the 1990s onward lead to other major entertainment tie-ins such as a Marvel superhero-themed amusement park at Universal Studios Orlando, and Batman-themed stunt shows and rollercoasters at Six Flags parks across America.

2000S

selected bibliography

Adobe History (timeline). Available from www.adobe.com/aboutadobe/pressroom/pdfs/timeline_090501.pdf; INTERNET.

Barfield, Ray. "Big Little Books." In *Handbook of American Popular Literature*, edited by M. Thomas Inge, 25–43. New York, Westport, Conn., and London: Greenwood Press, 1988.

Berry, W. Turner. "Printing and Related Trades." In *A History of Printing Technology*. Vol. 5, *The Late Nineteenth Century c. 1850–c. 1900*, edited by Charles Singer, E.J. Holmyard, A.R. Hall, and Trevor Williams, 683–715. Oxford: Clarendon Press, 1958.

Bindman, David. *Hogarth and His Times*. Berkeley and Los Angeles: University of California Press, 1997.

Blackbeard, Bill. *R.F. Outcault's The Yellow Kid: A Centennial Celebration of the Kid Who Started the Comics*. Northampton, Mass.: Kitchen Sink Press, 1995.

Blackbeard, Bill and Martin Williams, eds. *The Smithsonian Collection of Newspaper Comics*. Washington, D.C.: Smithsonian Institution Press; New York: Harry N. Abrams, Inc., 1977.

Bliss, Douglas Percy. *A History of Wood Engraving*. London: Spring Books, 1928, 1964.

Brown Shoe Company History and Timeline. Available from http://www.browngroup.com/history/index.asp; INTERNET.

Brynilden, J.C. "The Flash History." Available from http://www.flashmagazine.com; INTERNET.

Canemaker, John. *Felix: The Twisted Tale of the World's Most Famous Cat*. New York: Pantheon Books, 1991.

———. *Paper Dreams: The Art and Artists of Disney's Storyboards*. New York: Hyperion, 1999.

———. *Winsor McCay: His Life and Art*. New York: Abbeville Press, 1987.

Cerf, Vinton and Bernard Aboba. "How the Internet Came to Be" 1993. Available from www.internetvalley.com/archives/mirrors/cerf-how-inet.txt; INTERNET.

Cohen, Karl. "Milestones of the Animation Industry in the 20th Century." *Animation World Magazine* 4, no. 10 (January 2000). Available from http://mag.awn.com; INTERNET.

Cuno, James. "The Business and Politics of Caricature: Charles Philipon and La Maison Aubert." *Gazette des Beaux Arts* 6, no. 106 (October 1985): 95–112.

Donald, Diana. *The Age of Caricature: Satirical Prints in the Reign of George III*. New Haven and London: Yale University Press, 1996.

Dünnhaupt, Gerhard. "Sebastian Brant: The Ship of Fools." In *The Renaissance and Reformation in Germany: An Introduction*, 69–81. New York: Ungar, 1977.

Engen, Rodney. *Sir John Tenniel, Alice's White Knight*. Aldershot, Hants, England: Scolar Press; Brookfield, Vt., USA: Gower Publishing Co., 1991.

Gopnik, Adam. "A Critic at Large: The Man Who Invented Santa Claus—and His Evil Twin." *The New Yorker*, 15 December 1997, 84–98.

Gordon, Ian. *Comic Strips and Consumer Culture 1890–1945*. Washington, D.C., and London: Smithsonian Institution Press, 1998.

Heller, Steven. *Merz to Émigré and Beyond: Avant Garde Magazine Design of the Twentieth Century*. New York: Phaidon Press Inc., 2003.

Ivins, William M., Jr. *Prints and Visual Communication*. Vol. 10. Cambridge, Mass., and London: The MIT Press, 1969.

Jobling, Paul. "A Medium for the Masses I: The Popular Illustrated Weekly and the New Reading Public in France and England During the Nineteenth Century." In *Graphic Design: Reproduction and Representation since 1800*, 9–40. New York: Manchester University Press, 1996.

Kunzle, David. *History of the Comic Strip*. Vol. 2, *The Nineteenth Century*. Berkeley: University of California Press, c. 1990.

Le Beau, Bryan F. *Currier and Ives: America Imagined*. Washington, D.C., and London: Smithsonian Institution Press, 2001.

McCloud, Scott. *Understanding Comics: The Invisible Art*. New York: Harper Collins Publishers, Kitchen Sink Press, 1993.

McCloud, Scott. *Reinventing Comics*. New York: Harper Collins Publishers, 2000.

Roberts, Garyn G. *Dick Tracy and American Culture: Morality and Mythology, Text and Context*. Jefferson, N.C., and London: McFarland & Company, Inc., 1993.

Saff, Donald and Deli Sacilotto. *Printmaking History and Process*. New York: Holt, Rinehart and Wilson, 1978.

Spiegelman, Art and Chip Kidd. *Jack Cole and Plastic Man*. New York: DC Comics, 2001.

Wertham, Fredric. *Seduction of the Innocent*. New York: Rinehart and Company, Inc., 1954.

Wheeler, Doug, Robert L. Beerbohm, and Leonardo De Sá. "Töpffer in America." *Comic Art*, no. 3 (Summer 2003): 28–47.

Wright, Nicky. *The Classic Era of American Comics*. Chicago: Contemporary Books, 2000.

image credits

Dowd

R.F. Outcault, "The Yellow Kid Indulges in a Cockfight — A Waterloo," *The Yellow Kid*. Yellow Kid image courtesy of www.deniskitchen.com archives.

Winsor McCay, *Dream of the Rarebit Fiend*. Reprint permission granted by John Canemaker.

Promotional photograph for Brown Shoe Company associated with one of the **Buster Brown Comedies**. Image courtesy of Brown Shoe Company, Inc. © 1925–1929 Brown Shoe Company, Inc.

Otto Messmer and Pat Sullivan, Felix the Cat in *Feline Follies*. Felix the Cat is owned by Felix the Cat Productions Inc.

Otto Messmer and Pat Sullivan, *Felix the Cat: Big Little Book*. Image courtesy of Washington University Libraries, Department of Special Collections. Felix the Cat is owned by Felix the Cat Productions Inc. © 1936 Whitman Publishing Co.

Jay Ward and Bill Scott, "Peabody's Improbable History: Lucretia Borgia," *Rocky and Bullwinkle and Friends*, **episode 7**. Image reprinted with permission of Bullwinkle Studios. Licensed by Bullwinkle Studios, LLC. © 2004 Ward Productions, Inc.

Dan Zettwoch, *Ironclad: March 8th and 9th, 1862 A.D.* Image courtesy of Dan Zettwoch. © 2002 Dan Zettwoch.

John Porcellino, "Strange Skies," *King-Cat #1*. Image courtesy of John Porcellino. © 1989 John Porcellino.

Derek Kirk Kim, *Oliver Pikk #2*. Image courtesy of Derek Kirk Kim. © 2004 Derek Kirk Kim.

Luc Jacamon and Matz, Fons Schiedon, Submarine Channel, *The Killer*. Image courtesy of Submarine Channel. *The Killer—Long Feu* is © Casterman, Jacamon/Matz. *The Killer* is © 2001 Submarine.

Craig Frazier, "Greenville." Image courtesy of Craig Frazier. © 2002 Craig Frazier.

Demian Vogler, *When I Am King*, **chapter 1, scene 4**. Image courtesy of Demian Vogler. © 2000 Demian Vogler.

D.B. Dowd, *Holiday Moments with Cockeyed Neil*. Image courtesy of D.B. Dowd. Image and characters © 2000 Sam the Dog, Inc.

D.B. Dowd, *Sam the Dog in The Frame Job #78*, "The Arraignment" Image courtesy of D.B. Dowd. Image and characters © 1998 K9 & Moore.

Steve Whitehouse, *Mr. Man: Fishing*. Image courtesy of Steve Whitehouse. © 2003 Steve Whitehouse.

Lauren Redniss and Steven Guarnaccia, *Laman and Loay*. Image courtesy of Lauren Redniss. © 2003 Lauren Redniss.

Raeburn

Jack T. Chick, *The Beast*. Front cover reproduced by permission of Chick Publications. Website: www.chick.com. © 1988 Jack T. Chick LLC.

Jack T. Chick, *The Gay Blade*. Interior page 3 reproduced by permission of Chick Publications. Website: www.chick.com. © 1972, 2000 Jack T. Chick LLC.

Jack T. Chick, *Bewitched?*, German edition. Front cover reproduced by permission of Chick Publications. Website: www.chick.com. © 1972, 2001 Jack T. Chick LLC.

Jack T. Chick, *Soul Story*. Front cover reproduced by permission of Chick Publications. Website: www.chick.com. © 1977 Jack T. Chick LLC.

Jack T. Chick, *Bad Bob!* Front cover reproduced by permission of Chick Publications. Website: www.chick.com. © 1983 Jack T. Chick LLC.

Jack T. Chick, *Operation Bucharest*, **Crusaders Comic vol. 1**. Interior page reproduced by permission of Chick Publications. Website: www.chick.com. © 1974 Jack T. Chick LLC.

Chris Ware, Jimmy Corrigan, *The Smartest Kid on Earth*, *Magic Souvenir Book of Views*. Image courtesy of Chris Ware. © 1992 Chris Ware.

Heather Corcoran is assistant professor of Visual Communications at the School of Art at Washington University in St. Louis, and principal of Plum Studio. She builds information and brand systems, designs books, and writes articles related to visual culture and education. Her work can be seen at sweetplum.com.

D.B. Dowd is a professor of Visual Communications at the School of Art at Washington University in St. Louis. His animated murals, editorial illustration, visual books, and printmaking projects appear at ulcercity.com. His animated series **Sam the Dog** can be seen at samthedog.com.

Gerald Early is the Merle Kling Professor of Modern Letters in the English Department at Washington University in St. Louis. He is also the director of the Center for the Humanities for the College of Arts and Sciences. His latest book is **This Is Where I Came In: Black America in the 1960s** (University of Nebraska Press).

Todd Hignite is the founder, editor, and publisher of **Comic Art**, a publication devoted to all aspects of the comic medium, which won a 2004 Harvey Award. He has also worked as a critic, curator, and historian, and contributed an essay to the forthcoming anthology **The Education of a Cartoonist**, edited by Steven Heller.

Angela Miller teaches American arts and cultural history at Washington University. With five other authors, she has just completed **American Encounters: Art and Cultural Identity from the Beginning to the Present** (Prentice-Hall, forthcoming), an integrated survey of American arts which is the first of its kind to include coverage of the popular arts.

Daniel Raeburn writes and publishes **The Imp**, a series of odd booklets about comics. His essays have also appeared in **The Baffler**. He is the author of **The Art of Chris Ware**, which will be published in the fall of 2004 by Yale University Press.

editorial

D.B. Dowd
Editor

Todd Hignite
Editor

Sara Rowe Hignite
Copy Editor

Melanie Reinert
Researcher and
Assistant Editor

Shelley Edson
Research Assistant

Aaron Becker
Research Assistant

images

Melanie Reinert
Image Editor

Shelley Edson
Assistant Image Editor

design

Heather Corcoran
Creative Director, Designer

Stephanie Meier
Designer

Diana Seubert
Designer

Aaron Becker
Assistant Designer

exhibitions

The Rubber Frame: American Underground and Alternative Comics, 1964–2004
Des Lee Gallery

Todd Hignite
Curator

Philip Slein
Director, Des Lee Gallery

Tom Huck
Contributor

The Rubber Frame: The Visual Language of Comics from the Eighteenth Century to the Present
John M. Olin Library, Department of Special Collections

D.B. Dowd
Curator

Anne Posega
Director, Special Collections

Erin Davis
Curator of Rare Books, Special Collections

grants

Melinda Compton
Director of External Programs

The organizers of The Rubber Frame are pleased to acknowledge the support of the following organizations:

Missouri Arts Council
Regional Arts Commission

In addition, the following units of Washington University in St. Louis have made generous contributions:

Sam Fox Arts Center
School of Art
Visual Communications Area
College of Arts & Sciences
Center for the Humanities
American Culture Studies
*Olin Library, Department
    of Special Collections*

acknowledgments